## ACKNOWLEDGMENTS

I would like to thank all my colleagues, customers, family, friends, instructors and students (in alphabetical order). There are many to thank.

Many of the structures included in this book were designed by or are associated with individuals in the book arts who have provided me with both information and inspiration. I would like to thank Pauline Johnson (project two), Hedi Kyle (projects two, three, five and ten), Paul Johnson (projects one and five), Ed Hutchins (project one), Keith Smith and Bill Drendel.

I would also like to thank all the book artists and bookbinders who have contributed to the gallery sections, and Jennifer Long at North Light Books.

*to Andy*

# TABLE *of* CONTENTS

THE ESSENTIAL GUIDE TO MAKING

# HANDMADE *Books*

*Gabrielle Fox*

**NORTH LIGHT BOOKS**
CINCINNATI, OHIO
www.nlbooks.com

## ABOUT THE AUTHOR

Gabrielle Fox binds old and new books. She has exhibited widely and her books are in many public and private collections.

Gabrielle was born in the United States, where she received a degree in English Literature and Journalism. She traveled to the United Kingdom to study bookbinding, and since receiving her diploma in Fine Binding and Restoration nearly twenty years ago, has worked and taught in both the U.K. and the U.S.A. She is now living in Cincinnati, Ohio.

PHOTO BY BETH GILBERT

Other fine North Light Books are available from your local bookstore, art supply store or direct from the publisher.

04 03 02 01 00    5 4 3 2 1

**Library of Congress Cataloging-in-Publication Data**
Fox, Gabrielle
  The essential guide to making handmade books / Gabrielle Fox.
    p.cm.
  ISBN 1-58180-019-3 (pbk. : alk. paper)
   1. Bookbinding--Handbooks, manuals, etc. 2. Books--Handbooks, manuals, etc. I. Title
  Z271 .F78 2000
  686.3--dc21                                              00-024563

Edited by Jennifer Long
Production coordinated by John Peavler
Designed by Brian Roeth
Step-by-step photography by Christine Polomsky
Finished books photographed by Al Parrish

The permissions on page 125 constitute an extension of this copyright page.

# INTRODUCTION

*A* book opened reveals a world each of us interprets individually. We paint our own pictures from the descriptions and we create our own stories with the visual stimulation of colors and images. It is our very own world to keep, and only if we choose do we share the view or story we have experienced.

Books provide us with a space which can be put aside and reentered when we want to continue the story, remember a person or express ourselves. What a wonderful thing to share and what a delightful way to express yourself!

The projects I demonstrate in this book provide a progression of skills and techniques as you go from project one through eleven. The first project requires only a half sheet of paper and a few drawing and cutting tools. As you move through the different structures and become comfortable with the materials you are using, you will learn various sewing techniques and begin to glue things together. The final project is a simple container which will be easiest to master if you use the measuring skills you have acquired while making the other projects.

Gabrielle Fox in her studio.

However, each project has been explained fully so that you can choose any project in the book and get started right there. If there are any terms or tools which you are not familiar with, just refer to the explanations and definitions at the beginning of the book and you will be able to keep going without difficulty.

I hope you enjoy making the books and containers described and shown here and find the artists' and binders' books in the gallery exciting and helpful in creating even more books of your own.

# CHAPTER 1

# hand tools

These are the tools you will need to make your own books. Most are available at craft and art supply stores. If you can't find any of these tools in your area, see the list of suppliers on page 124.

**Bodkin or Awl and Chisel** Use the bodkin or awl for punching round holes. A large needle will also work. A woodworker's chisel will enable you to make a straight-line cut into a board when you want to run ribbons through it for ties.

**Bone Folder** A letter opener-shaped piece of bone which provides a smooth surface with which to fold and score paper. There are Teflon bone folders now available. You can also use the plastic sewing tool used to push out the corners in a collar, or similarly-shaped wooden pottery tools.

**Cutting Mat** A self-healing cutting mat or a piece of board will protect the surface of your workspace.

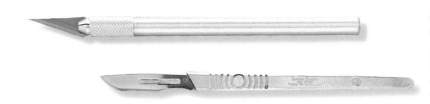

**Scalpel or Small Craft Knife** You will want a knife with disposable blades that can be changed when dull. Use the scalpel or craft knife to cut paper and lighter materials. Scalpel blade no. 11 is straight to the point and no. 10 is rounded to the point.

**Heavier Craft Knife** Use this for cutting board

**Long, Flat-Bladed Knife** Use to cut folded paper into sheets.

**Scissors** It's good to have both a small pair and a large pair of scissors. Pinking shears are good for creating decorative edges.

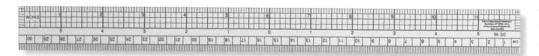

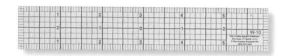

**Plastic Ruler** Use for measuring. Use the metal ruler for cutting as the plastic ruler flexes and you can cut slivers off the ruler easily.

**Metal Ruler** Use for measuring and as a straight edge to cut along when cutting with a knife.

**Metal Triangle or Set Square** Metal edges are always preferable to cut against or use as a guide when cutting.

**Spring or Set Dividers** These are metal dividers that stay open to a measurement you have set so you can use that measurement while you are working. This is often quicker than measuring with a ruler. For bookbinding you want the straight leg dividers.

**Plastic Triangle** The larger plastic triangles are made of fairly sturdy plastic and can be cut against, but be careful not to start cutting bits of plastic off them.

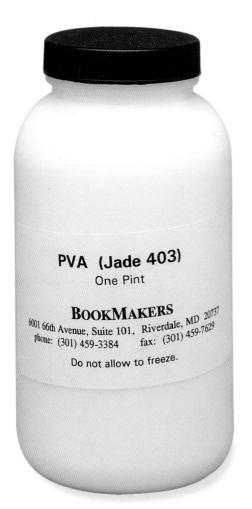

**Glue, Brush and Container**
PVA or white glue comes in various formulas. The most common glues used in bookmaking are Jade 403 or wheat starch paste, although Sobo or YES paste can be used. Glue should be applied with a brush—any brush will work as long as you wash it out well between uses and choose the right size for the job. I recommend pouring a bit of glue into a bowl or small container rather than working directly from the bottle. This way you can easily thin the glue with water if it feels too thick and doesn't brush smoothly.

**Felt Tip Marker** Permanent felt tip markers work well for adding designs and lettering to your projects, but anything you prefer to use is fine, including paints.

**Mechanical Pencil and Eraser** A fairly soft lead will erase easily and a no. 5 or no. 7 lead in a mechanical pencil will give a fine enough line for drawing measurements and positioning lines. I prefer to use solid white Staedtler or Koh-I-Nor erasers when removing marks from my paper.

# terminology & techniques

*Parts of a Book*

**head** – top

**spine** – The area where all the pages are gathered or sewn together.

**Foredge** – Where the pages open out; opposite of spine.

**wrapper** – A lightweight, folded cover.

**tail** – bottom

**boards** – The front and back of the case or cover.

**joint** – The point at which the spine and the front and back covers hinge.

**case** – Another name for the cover.

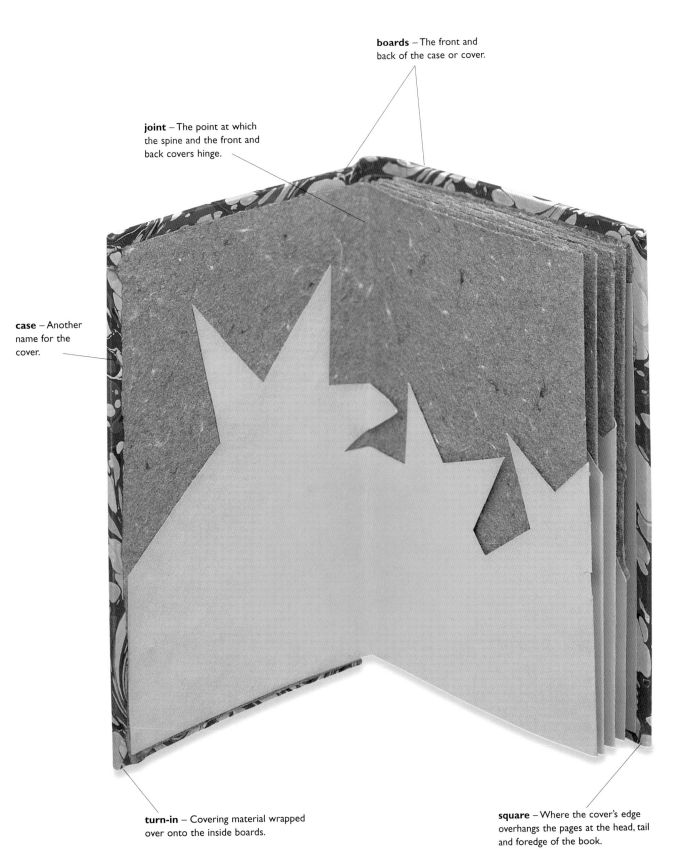

**turn-in** – Covering material wrapped over onto the inside boards.

**square** – Where the cover's edge overhangs the pages at the head, tail and foredge of the book.

## Grain Direction

Machine-made paper and board both have a grain, or direction of greater strength. When the paper and board are made, the fibers are pulled more in one direction than the other, which lines the fibers up with more strength in one direction than the other.

Handmade paper has very little grain direction because the sheets are formed individually in a wooden frame or mold and deckle and there is no strong pulling to align the fibers in one direction.

Cloth also has a direction of strength, or warp. When cloth is woven, there are threads which are pulled tight in one direction while the threads going in the other direction are woven in and out of the warp threads. The easiest way to remember the warp of cloth is that the warp runs parallel to the selvage of the cloth and the warp threads are the straightest ones.

It is always a good idea to test the grain of all the materials you are using to be certain your materials are working together and you will get the best results from them.

### TESTING THE GRAIN IN PAPER AND BOARD

The simplest way to find the grain direction of paper is to fold it gently in half and feel the resistance. If you can't feel much difference, close your eyes and test it again. If it still isn't clear, wet a corner of the paper and it will curl more in one direction than the other. The direction it curls in is the weakest and therefore the grain is going in the opposite or strongest direction.

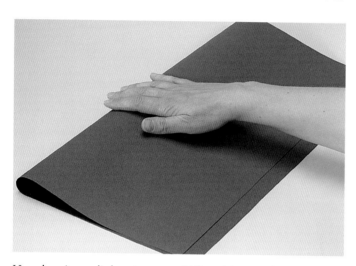

Here there is very little resistance to folding; this is not the grain direction.

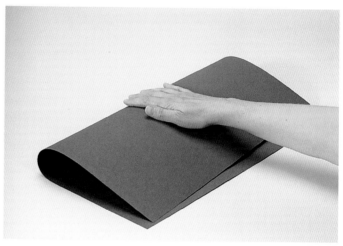

There is more resistance as I fold in this direction. When I lay this sheet of paper flat, the grain will go in the direction of my arm.

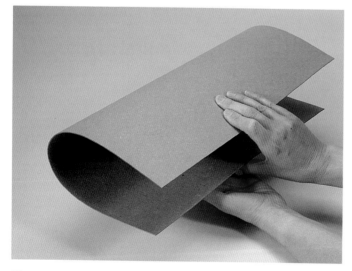

There is very little resistance when I flex the board in this direction.

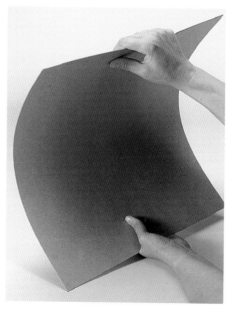

There is much more resistance when I flex the board in this direction; the grain is running up and down the length of this board.

### Testing Acidity in Paper and Board

Acidity in paper and board will cause them to deteriorate. Old paper which has turned yellow and is very brittle to the touch is high in acid content. High alkalinity—the opposite pH level—can cause other problems, so ideally the acid and alkaline level should be balanced at about pH 7.0. Making your books with acid-neutral materials and storing them in well ventilated areas away from direct sunlight will help them last longer.

### Cutting a Straight Edge

To cut a straight line, you will need a ruler or triangle to provide a straight edge as the guide for your knife. Always use a heavier knife for heavier board—a small knife blade can easily snap. A series of light strokes creates a much cleaner and straighter cut than one heavy dig.

Always cut a straight edge along the top of the material you're using before measuring or cutting to size.

### Cutting a Right Angle

Line your triangle up against the straight cut you have just made and use it as a guide to give you a 90° angle. Remember, a series of light strokes with your knife will give you a cleaner cut.

A pH pen can be purchased at any major art supply shop and is the easiest way to test the acidity of paper and board if you want to be certain your materials are acid free. The pen will come with directions, but basically when you draw a line on the material the chlorophenol red solution will turn the mark yellow or colorless if the pH is less than 6.8, which means the paper is acidic. The mark will turn purple if the pH is 6.8 or above, which means the paper is acid free.

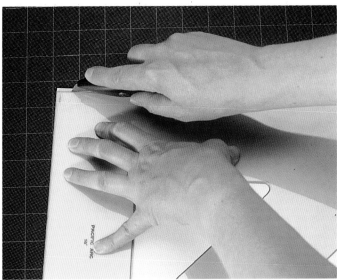

Cutting a straight edge.

Now that I know the left edge is straight, I can line the triangle up with it and cut a right angle along the opposite side of the triangle.

# CHAPTER 3

# step-by-step projects

# SIMPLE TUNNEL BOOK

*A* single sheet of paper, really half a sheet of paper, is the only material you need in order to make this first project. If you find you'd rather create a garden or a corridor than a maze, this project is straightforward enough that you can design your own simple tunnel from the beginning.

Read through the directions so that once you've folded and cut the paper, the pages open in the direction you want them to. This is simple, but even folding and cutting can get better with practice.

The simple tunnel book can be a card, keepsake or full book with a complete story to share. This structure can be delightfully simple or packed tight with information and detail.

## WHAT YOU'LL NEED

• One 8½" × 5½" (21.6cm × 14cm) sheet of paper (half of a sheet of traditional stationery). I used Hammermill Cover, Brite Hue which comes in a pack of 125 sheets of assorted colors and is 65 lb. (80gsm). This green color is from the more traditional color pack.

• bodkin or needle

• bone folder

• clear plastic ruler or straightedge

• cutting mat

• felt tip marker

• mechanical pencil

• scissors

• small craft knife or scalpel

• small triangle

• white eraser

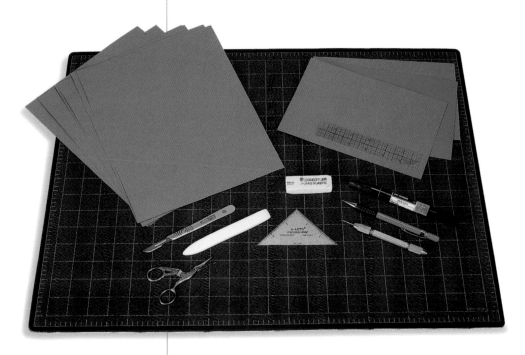

*1* Fold the sheet of paper in half lengthwise. Match up the two upper lefthand corners and the two edges first. Hold the paper in position firmly with one hand and then rub the flat end of the bone folder gently along the side to be folded.

*2* Open the sheet up and then fold it in half widthwise.

*3* Fold the top flap back on itself to meet with the fold you have just made. Rub the new fold down gently with the flat side of the bone folder.

*4* Flip the sheet over and fold the other flap back on itself to meet with the center fold.

*Hint*

*Print up an invitation with directions or write a short holiday story for a card, then make copies on a computer printer or copying machine and fold them into tunnel books.*

*5* Open the folded sheet and you will find you have folded eight equal squares. Position the sheet on the cutting surface so that the center fold is peaked up, as in the photograph.

*6* With your craft knife and a straightedge or ruler, cut lengthwise along the first three squares on the center fold.

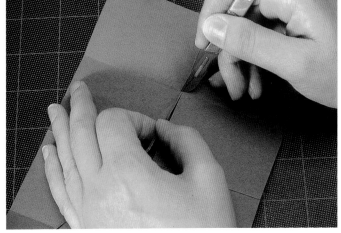

*7* Just below the first cut, make another cut the same length. Cut the resulting thin strip of paper off at the end.

This is the basic structure before any detail or decoration is added.

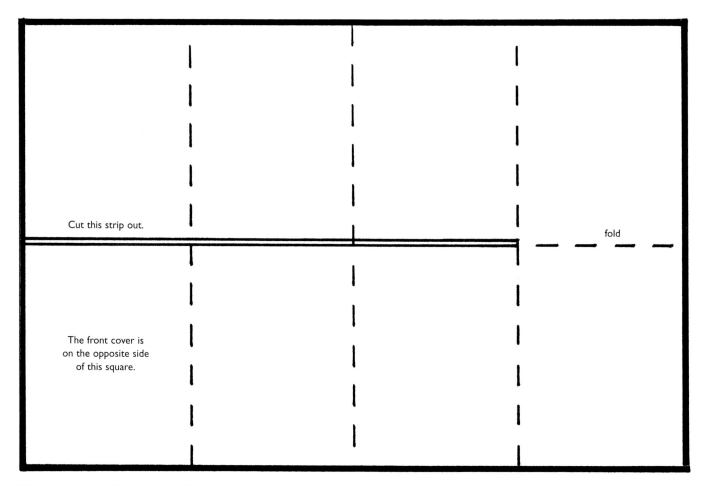

Cut this strip out.

fold

The front cover is
on the opposite side
of this square.

This diagram shows how the tunnel book is folded and cut.

*8* Fold in the bottom four squares like an accordion. The back of the furthest left square is the front cover (see the diagram above). Fold the first square over the second square, the second square under the third square and the third square over the fourth square. The title of my tunnel book is *Mazes.* Write in a title for your book using a black marker. Add other artwork if you wish.

*9* Here I've opened the bottom four squares back up and drawn in some simple mazes. The round squiggle is on the opposite side of the front cover square. The square and triangle mazes are on the second and third squares.

*10* Flip the sheet of paper over. In the top right square, use a pencil to begin drawing an outline for whatever you would like to cut out. Remember that this is the first of three (if you would like a solid background on the last page) or four cut-out pages and you will want to look through this one, down into the tunnel. I've drawn a bush on the right side; the opening will be on the left.

*11* Cut out the opening and use a white rubber eraser to erase any pencil marks which are unnecessary.

*12* Flip the sheet over. Fold the first page (with the cut-out) over the second. Trace around the opening on the first page through to the second in order to line up the images.

*13* A needle or bodkin can be used to mark a point to line up areas which can't be seen through the first window, such as the lower right corner covered by the bush.

*14* Open the first page back up. Draw the next panel design, then cut out the second window. This is a bush on the left side with a window on the righthand side. When opened out, it appears that the bushes in the first and second squares are on the same side, but when the first page is folded over the second, one bush will be on the right and one will be on the left. Cut the third panel as you did the first panel (with a righthand bush). Cut the fourth panel as you did the second panel (with a lefthand bush).

*15* If you'd like, you may draw a dotted line on the fourth square (next to the triangle maze) to show how the folded panels telescope out to become a tunnel.

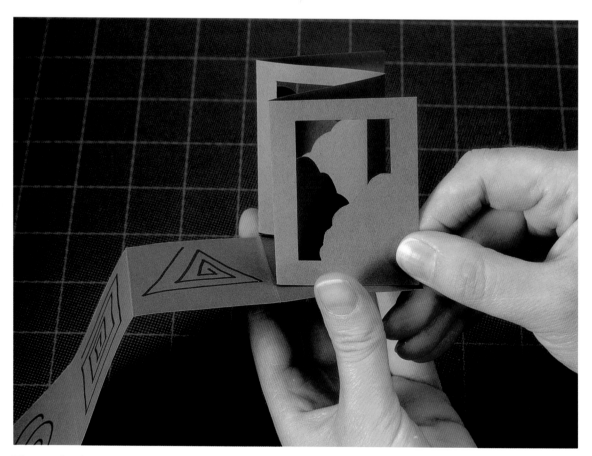

The completed maze.

# GALLERY *of* IDEAS

## Tunnel O' Love
Edward H. Hutchins
color copied panels mounted on cardstock with Fabriano hinges; 4" × 5" (10.2cm × 12.7cm)

This is a different tunnel structure to consider. The simplest way to begin this tunnel is to cut out and decorate the boards first. They can be attached to one another by folding 2 inch (5.1cm) wide pieces of paper into four-panel accordions. Glue the first panel to the back of the first board and the last panel to the front of the next board. Repeat on both sides and you will form an accordion all the way to the back board.

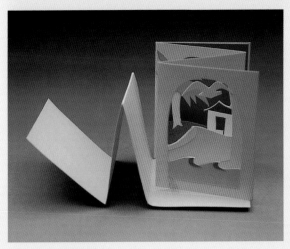

## Pretty in Pink
Elizabeth Koffel
colored card; 4" × 3" (10.2cm × 7.6cm)

Cutouts of different colored card have been glued to the panels of this accordion to form an island scene.

## Peep Show Book
Paul Johnson
watercolor paper and dyes; 6" × 3¼" (15.2cm × 8.3cm)

Here the standing accordion has been folded in the other direction so that the tunnel folds out and away from the first half of the book. Dyes are used to achieve these deep, rich colors.

# NON-ADHESIVE ACCORDION BOOK

he first portable books were clay tablets. Letters known as Cuneiform—developed by the Sumerians in about 3500 B.C.—were drawn into the clay before it was baked in the sun or in an oven.

The earliest widely-known material to be written *on* rather than *in* was papyrus. To make papyrus scrolls, strips from the inner stem of the papyrus plant were laid flat and layered vertically and horizontally on top of one another, then pressed together.

In order to find information in the center of a scroll, you have to unroll it. Perhaps that's one reason why scroll users began folding the papyrus back and forth on itself in an accordion fashion. This made it easier to turn to the page in the middle. A more practical reason may have been that a folded document with a cover or weight on top was easier to store.

This non-adhesive accordion (or concertina) is made of a folded strip of paper whose ends slide into a cover made of two pieces of thin board and more folded paper.

There is no gluing because the pieces all fit together snugly and hold one another in place.

## WHAT YOU'LL NEED

- One sheet of Crescent drawing paper—I used Williamsburg Green—which is 22" × 32"(55.9cm × 81.3cm) and 80 lb. (170gsm). You will only use about half of the sheet of paper.

- marbled or other decorative paper which is at least stationery weight

- two pieces of lightweight board, or a single sheet which is ⅛-inch (0.14cm) to ¼-inch (0.18cm) thick

- bone folder (both Teflon and natural bone shown here)

- cutting mat

- heavy craft knife

- large triangle

- mechanical pencil

- scissors

- small craft knife or scalpel

- straightedge

- strips of paper or a ruler (for measuring)

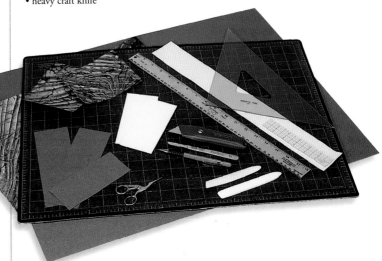

## *Hint*

*You can use lightweight wrapping paper in place of the marbled or decorative paper. Reinforce the gift wrap by sticking tape on the reverse side at the edges so the paper will not tear. A conservation-quality tape is best, but a good clear tape will also work, as long as you understand it won't last indefinitely.*

*1* Mark the height of the book you want to make on a piece of scrap paper. I made this book six inches (15.2cm) high. Use the piece of scrap paper to mark the measurement in several places along the length of the sheet you are cutting.

*2* Place a straightedge on the marks you have just made and cut along the marks with a small craft knife or scalpel. This long strip of paper will be the body of your book.

*3* Cut the corners at right angles using a plastic triangle and craft knife or scalpel.

*4* Fold the piece of paper in half widthwise. To do this, line up the two free edges first. After you have the paper in position, hold it in place with one hand and rub down the fold with the flat end of the bone folder.

## Hint

*When you want to cut a square edge, always start by first cutting straight across the top length of the material. This assures you that you have one straight edge. Now line your triangle up with that edge and cut your square edge or corner.*

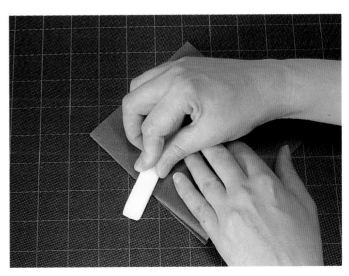

*5* Fold the upper flap back on itself, lining up the free edge with the center fold you just made. Rub the fold down gently with the flat end of the bone folder.

*6* Flip the sheet over and fold the other flap back on itself to meet with the center fold.

*7* Now fold the top flap back on itself again to meet with the fold you made in step six. Rub this fold down.

*8* Flip the book over and fold the other flap back on itself to meet with the fold you made in step five.

At this stage, when opened up, your book should look like this.

*9* Place the book down on the work surface so that the center fold is open and smaller folded flaps are facing the work surface. Fold the righthand page back on itself to meet with the center fold and gently rub it down. The previous folds will now be on top.

*10* Now fold the lefthand page back on itself to meet with the center fold and gently rub it down.

*11* Pick the book up and fold it at the center line to form an accordion.

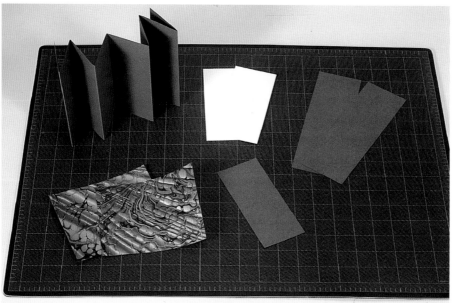

These are all of the pieces you will need to assemble this project. You have folded your accordion. Next you will cut out two boards (the white pieces). Then you will measure and cut the pieces of paper for covering the boards and spine.

*12* Cut a corner of the cover board square. This will give you a straight edge to measure against.

*13* Check the grain of the board. The grain should run from the head of the book to the tail, not across the width. Starting at the straight edge you just cut, mark the exact height and width of the folded accordion onto the cover board. If you would like a square (where the cover extends past the inner pages), add the extra measurement at the head, tail and foredge only; you will not have a square at the spine. Now move the book to the edge of the last measurement and mark the measurement again. You will be cutting two boards of the same size.

*14* Line the triangle up with the board edge and cut along the height of both book boards. Hold the triangle firmly with one hand and cut the board with a heavy utility knife.

*15* Use the same technique to cut the boards to width, creating two identical pieces of board.

*16* Now we'll cut two pieces of paper for the outside of the covers. I'm using marbled paper for my book. Remember to always measure from a squared-off corner, and check the grain of the paper. The grain should go from head to tail. Place one of the boards you cut in the last step on the reverse side and against the squared off corner of the front cover paper (my marbled paper is plain on the back). Mark the exact height of the board onto the paper. When marking the width of the board, add two inches (5.1cm). Repeat these measurements for the second piece. Cut these two pieces of paper as you cut the boards. A small craft knife or scalpel will be strong enough to cut through the paper.

*17* For the inside of the covers, measure, mark and cut two pieces of paper which are the exact width of the book boards, and the height of the book boards plus two inches (5.1cm). I'm using green Crescent drawing paper.

*18* Measure, mark and cut one spine piece which is the exact height of the book and the depth of the book plus two inches.

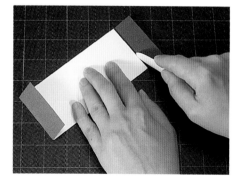
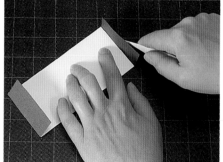
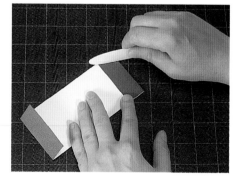

*19* Lay a cover board in the center of an inside cover piece. Run the tip of the bone folder along each edge, making a slight groove—this is called scoring and will help make a clean fold. Now score along the outside of the paper to help it fold. Fold the extra inch (2.5cm) of paper at either end over the edge of the board and smooth with the flat edge of the bone folder. Repeat for the other cover board.

*20* Cut off the corners of the paper ⅟₁₆-inch (0.16cm) to ⅛-inch (0.3cm) down from the fold. This will give the paper some strength and space to anchor in over the edge of the board. Cutting off the corner edge of the paper makes it easier to fold in and less likely to bunch up against the front cover paper.

*21* Remove the inside cover papers from the boards. Use the procedure from step 19 to fold the outside cover papers (the marbled paper) around the book boards widthwise. Trim off the corners as you did in step 20.

*22* Cut off one-third of the first and last panels of the accordion.

*23* Cut off the corners of these panels.

*24* Mark the width of the spine on a scrap of paper. This measurement should not be too tight or the book will fan out at the foredge because it will be too constricted at the spine. However, don't go to the opposite extreme and make it too wide, either.

*25* Transfer this measurement to the center top of the spine piece which you cut out earlier.

*26* Line the plastic triangle up with the mark you just made and score and fold the paper up against the edge of the triangle.

*27* Trim the corners off. Remember to trim them just away from the folded edge.

*28* The first step in assembling the book is to wrap the outside cover around each book board.

*29* Hook the top flap of the inside cover paper in between the outside cover and the book board. Place the inside paper on top of the outside paper's flaps and slot the bottom flap of the inside paper in at the other end of the board.

*30* Slide one end of the accordion in underneath the inside cover paper so that it tucks in neatly against the edge of the board.

*31* Holding everything in place, slide the other cover in.

*32* The final step is to slide each flap of the spine piece in between the accordion and the two covers.

# GALLERY *of* IDEAS

## Souvenirs of Great Cities
Dorothy A. Yule; illustrations by Susan Hunt Yule
letterpress printed on Mohawk Superfine Cover
2½" × 2½" × ¾" (6.4cm × 6.4cm × 1.9cm)

Each small book in this boxed set has two spines that can be removed one at a time to open up one side of the story. Removing both spines allows the books to "accordion" out to their full lengths.

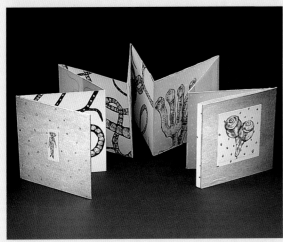

## *Janus*
Kate Kern
black pen on watercolor paper; white paint on
metallic paper-covered boards
5½" × 5½"(14cm × 14cm); extends to
55 inches (140cm)

This accordion's cover is made up of a board attached at each end. There is also a piece of watercolor paper that is attached to the front board and wraps from underneath and across the folded back to flap under the back board. There are no rules as long as it fits!

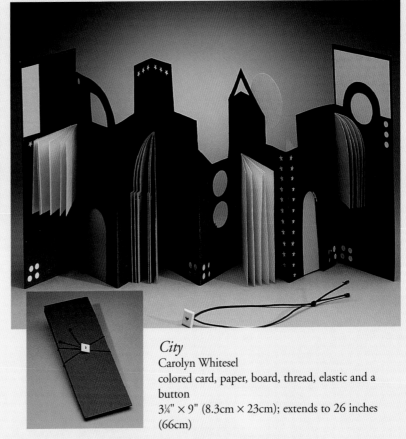

## *City*
Carolyn Whitesel
colored card, paper, board, thread, elastic and a
button
3¼" × 9" (8.3cm × 23cm); extends to 26 inches
(66cm)

This city is a shaped accordion with cutouts, punched holes and shaped, sewn-in signatures. The closure is made with covered elastic and a button.

# ACCORDION ALBUM

Any book can be made into an album. You just need to include tabs or spacers at the spine to compensate for the thickness of whatever you want to stick into the album. Otherwise, the book will fan out as you put your photos and memorabilia into it.

This structure can be made in any size. As it gets larger, it will get floppier unless you use heavier paper or card. In this example, you will cut out windows to compensate for the additions rather than insert spacers at the spine.

If you can't find any postage stamps that appeal to you for this project, or want a different look, you can also use cancelled stamps, stickers, old advertisement or wine labels, or you can draw something yourself and use glue to adhere it.

## WHAT YOU'LL NEED

• One yellow, two orange and three lime green sheets of Hammermill Cover, Brite Hue which comes in a pack of 125 sheets of assorted colors and is 65 lb. (180gsm). The colors I used for this project come in the fluorescent color pack. All of the sheets you will be using in this project are 8½" × 5½" (21.6cm × 14cm). Cut the full size sheets in half to get this measurement.

• Two sheets of four larger postage stamps. The U.S. Post Office comes out with different, wonderful stamps every month.

• bone folder (both Teflon and natural bone shown here)

• card or paper for templates

• clear plastic ruler

• cutting mat

• large triangle

• mechanical pencil

• PVA glue, brush and container

• scrap paper

• small craft knife or scalpel

• small L-square

• spring dividers

## *Hint*

*If you'd like to turn a book you already have into an album, cut out most of every other page, leaving just a strip near the spine. This is done most easily if you place a thin piece of board, such as the piece at the back of a pad of paper, under the page you want to cut and then push a metal ruler into the gutter of the book to cut against. This will give you the same size tabs or spacers all through the book. This thickness at the spine will balance out the additional thickness in the pages added by the things you insert into the album.*

*1* Line up the edges of one full sheet of paper as if you were going to fold it in half, but just make a slight crease at the center top.

*2* With a craft knife or scalpel, cut the sheet of paper in half at the mark you just made, using a plastic triangle as a guide. Repeat this procedure to cut three more sheets of paper in half.

*3* Fold six of the eight pieces of paper you just cut in half width-wise. One piece is for the accordion spine, two are for the front and back covers and three are for the pages in the middle. The other two pieces will not be used.

*4* Choose one piece of paper for the spine. This piece will be folded many times in order to form the accordion spine to which the covers and inside folded sheets are attached. Place the sheet down on the work surface with the folded edge to your left. Bring the free edge (the right edge) of the top flap back to the center fold on your left. Rub down the new fold with your bone folder, taking care to hold the paper firmly in place.

*5* Flip the paper over and fold the other flap back on itself to meet with the center fold.

*6* Now fold the free edge on your left back to meet with the fold on the right. Rub this fold down.

*7* Place the sheet down on the work surface so that the center fold is open and the smaller folded panels on the right are facing the work surface. Fold the right half of the sheet back on itself so that the free edge of the smaller folded panels meets with the center fold. Rub down with the bone folder.

*8* Flip the sheet over, keeping the smaller folds to the right. Now fold the narrower top flap back on itself to meet with the fold on the left. Press down.

*9* Flip the sheet over again and fold the left half back on itself to meet the center fold. The smaller folds will now be on top. Rub down the fold with the bone folder.

*Hint*

*You can review the procedure for folding an accordion in project two.*

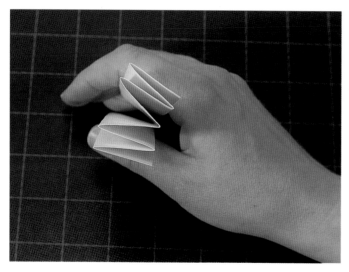

*10* Pick up the piece of paper and fold the two halves under at the center fold to form an accordion.

*11* Choose two of the sheets you folded in step three for the covers. Open each to the inside and draw a pencil line about ½-inch (1.3cm) in on both edges. This line is a guide which will make it easier to position the cover when you glue it to the accordion spine.

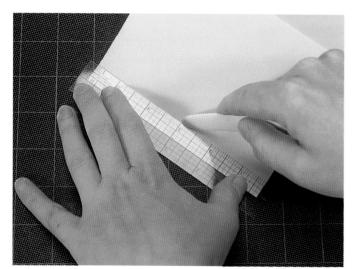

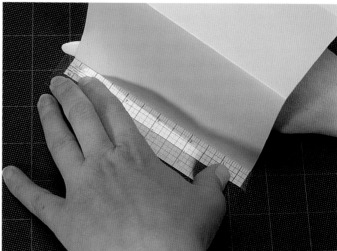

*12* Score and fold the free edges of the three inside pages which will attach to the spine the same amount as you marked on the covers. This will allow them to flex more easily.

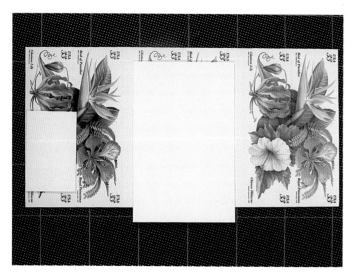

*13* Make templates from card the exact size and shape of the windows you want in the album. My album has one window which will show the full set of four stamps. The smaller windows will show each stamp individually. Make your windows the appropriate size for the stamps or other artwork you'll be displaying in your album.

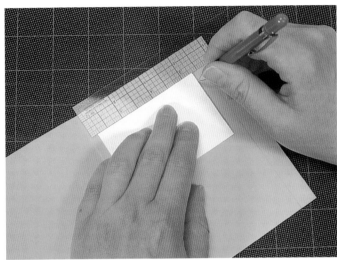

*14* Position the templates on each page to decide where you want the windows to go. Be sure that your windows will fit on the page with a margin all around; you don't want your window disappearing into the spine or running off the edge of the page.

*15* Open the pages up and trace around the template with a pencil. Always check your measurements one more time before cutting.

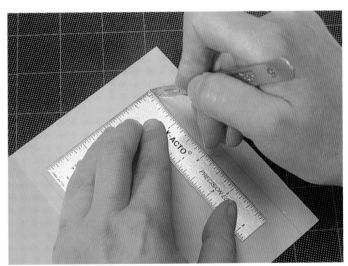

*16* Cut the windows out from the inside. Use a small craft knife or scalpel and a small straightedge or triangle to keep the cuts straight and square.

*17* Close the pages and lightly outline the windows in pencil onto the inside of the page.

*18* Position the stamps within the penciled guides and attach. Erase any pencil marks which are still visible.

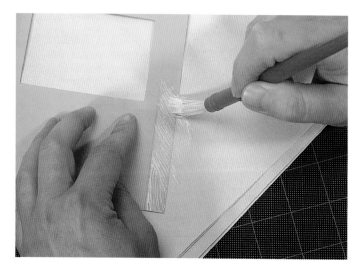

*19* Attach the back cover first as a guide. You are building toward the front of the album. Use the glue brush to apply glue to both inner edges of the back cover, up to the pencil marks you made earlier.

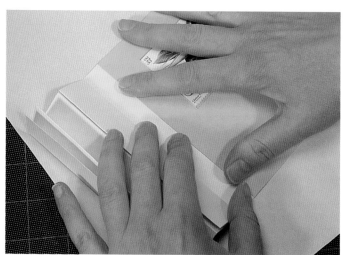

*20* While holding the back cover open, position the end of the accordion spine on top of the left inside edge of the cover, lining it up to the pencil mark and onto the glued edge. Rub the edge down gently. Fold the righthand side of the page down on top of the end of the spine and rub down.

*21* Glue the inside of the next page's edge to the next fold of the spine. Line up the fold on the edge of the page with the fold on the accordion spine. Fold the top half of the page down so that it meets and rub down gently. Attach the remaining pages to the spine in the same manner. Attach the front cover as you did the back.

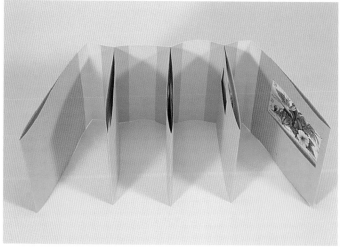

*22* Stand the album up for half an hour and let it dry a bit before folding it up.

# GALLERY *of* IDEAS

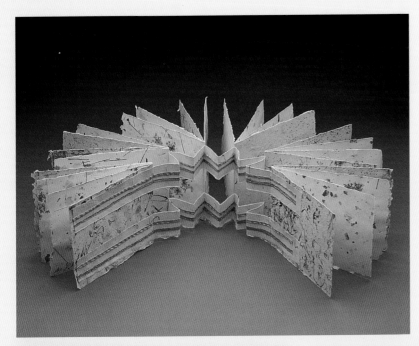

## Garden Mix
Margaret Rhein
Terrapin Paper Mill handmade cotton paper with flower inclusions, ribbon and thread
4½" × 6" (11.4cm × 15.2cm)

The sections of this book are sewn to the two accordion strips.

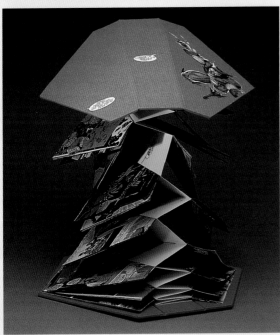

## Apart From Being Flippant, What Are You Doing Here?
William Drendel
cloth covered boards, card, thread and comic book pages
approximately 6" × 6" (15.2cm × 15.2cm)

This hexagonal book has hinged covers and a card accordion which runs from front to back or top to bottom. The shaped pages are sewn to the accordion.

## Green and Pink Paste Paper
Virginia Wisniewski
card and hand-decorated paste paper
8" × 5" (20.3cm × 12.7cm)

The folded pages in this book are glued together and the book slides into the cover described in project two.

# JACOB'S LADDER

*K*nown as Jacob's Ladders, or earlier as click tablets, these structures were often used as educational tools for children as far back as the eighteenth century. If you hold one end up and get the first panel to flop down it will set off a chain reaction all down the book. Turn it over and do the same to get another set of images, all appearing to be connected with three pieces of ribbon.

## *Hint*

*Traditionally, small panels of wood have been used to make this structure. You can use wood blocks in place of the board if you would prefer. If you use thick pieces of wood, make the ribbons longer.*

### WHAT YOU'LL NEED

- ten scraps of decorative paper which are 1¾" × 2" (4.5cm × 5.1cm) or larger

- Ten postage stamps. The floral ones I am using came in a little package of ten first-class stamps and twenty greeting labels and were designed by Tutssels for the Royal Mail in England. You can use any stamps or decals, decorative paper, photos or your own artwork.

- Five pieces of card or wood which are 2⅛" wide × 1⅝" high (5.4cm × 4.1cm). I used a four-ply acid-free card which is a little softer and easier to cut than traditional board.

- pieces of ribbon cut to ⅜" wide × 4" long (1cm × 10.2cm), which is about twice the width of the pieces of card:
    four pieces of rainbow-colored ribbon
    two pieces of blue ribbon
    two pieces of orange ribbon
    two pieces of pink ribbon
    two pieces of yellow ribbon

- bone folder

- heavy craft knife

- large triangle

- mechanical pencil

- pinking shears

- PVA glue, brush and container

- scrap paper

- small scissors

- two small weights

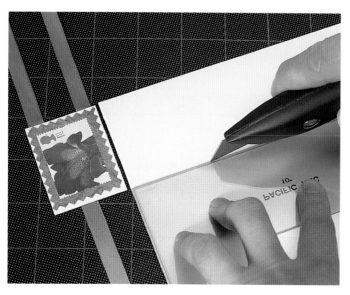

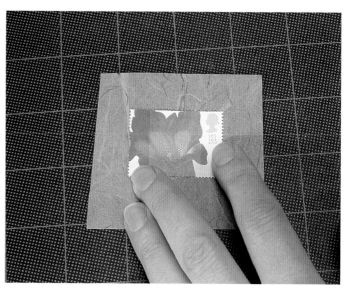

*1* Cut six identical pieces of heavy card or board. I sized mine to accomodate the bordered postage stamps (see steps two and three) I chose for this project. Always use a heavier knife when cutting board. If you cut a long strip that is the right height, as in the photo, you can easily cut the strip into pieces the correct width.

*2* Stick each stamp to a piece of colored or decorative paper larger than the stamp.

*3* Trim around the edges of the stamps with a pair of pinking shears, leaving a border of decorative paper around the stamp.

*4* Cut four pieces of multicolored ribbon and two pieces each of yellow, pink, orange and blue ribbon. Cut each length of ribbon twice the width of the pieces of board.

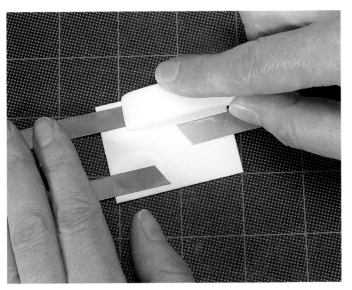

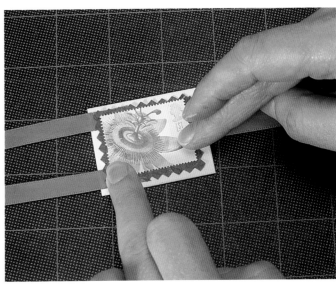

*5* Glue one multicolored ribbon to a piece of board with its tail to your right. Glue two blue ribbons to the other edge of the board with their tails to the left. The single multicolored ribbon should be centered vertically and ½-inch (1.3cm) in from the edge. The two blue ribbons should be about ⅟₁₆-inch (0.12cm) from the edge of the board; glue one at the top and one at the bottom.

*6* Glue a bordered stamp over the ribbons so that the flower is right side up when facing you, with the single ribbon to your right.

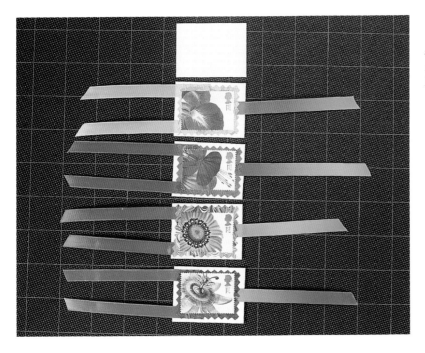

*7* Assemble the five pieces to this Jacob's Ladder as shown. With the stamps right side up, all the single ribbons are going to the right as with the first panel. The last panel is left blank at this point.

*Hint*

*I've left the back of the first panel blank so that you can see when the Jacob's Ladder is flipped from the front to the back during assembly. If you would prefer, flip the first panel over with the two blue ribbons to your right and attach the bordered stamp right side up to the back now.*

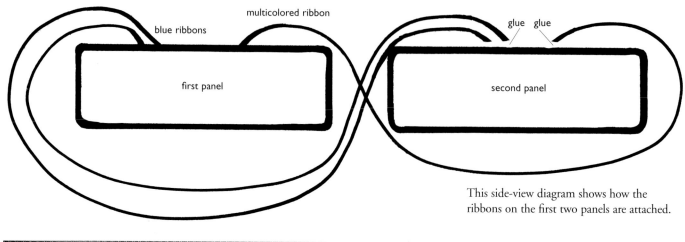

This side-view diagram shows how the ribbons on the first two panels are attached.

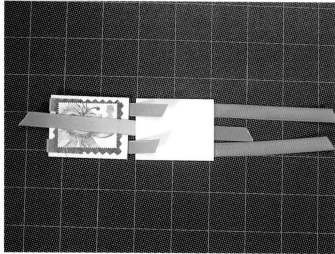

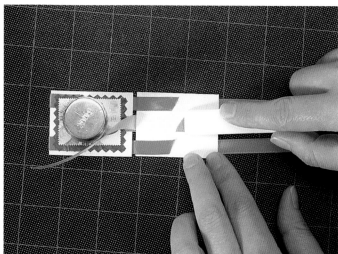

*8* Place the first panel down on the work surface with the two blue ribbons on your left, just as it was positioned in step seven. Fold the blue ribbons under the panel so that the two short blue tails are now visible to the right. Place the second panel down to the right of the first panel. Leave enough space between them so that the ladder will flip easily. This space should be at least twice the thickness of the board used for the panels. Position the second panel so that it is on top of the first panel's multicolored ribbon (only the blue tip of it is showing here) and the two short blue tails come up and onto the top of the second panel. Glue the two blue ribbons down to the second panel.

*9* Fold the multicolored tail from the first panel back over the right-hand edge of the second panel and glue it down. Placing a small weight on the first panel will help keep things from sliding around as you work.

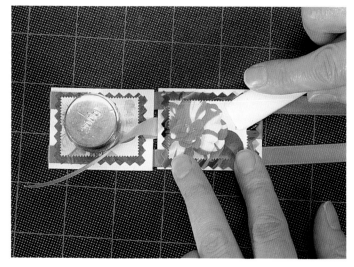

*10* Glue a bordered stamp to the second panel on top of the three ribbon ends.

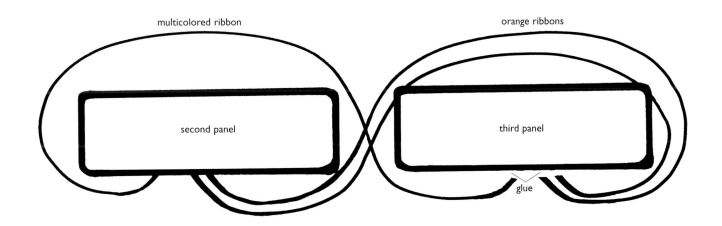

multicolored ribbon                    orange ribbons

second panel                           third panel

glue

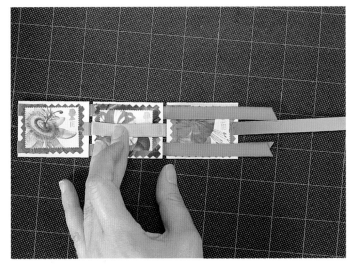

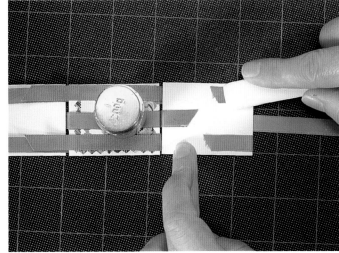

*11* Line up the third panel to the right of the second, with the flower right side up and the second panel's orange ribbons across the top of the third panel. Fold the two pink ribbons on the left of the third panel underneath, as you did with the first panel. The center multicolored ribbon from the left side of the second panel will run across the front of the second panel and will tuck under the left side of the third panel.

*12* Flip all three panels over and glue the tail of the second panel's multicolored ribbon to the left edge of the third panel. Glue the tails of the two orange ribbons to the right edge.

*13* Glue a bordered stamp to the third panel over the glued ends of ribbon. Since you are working on the back side of the panels and this side faces the opposite direction, the stamp should be upside down, just like the stamp on this side of the second panel.

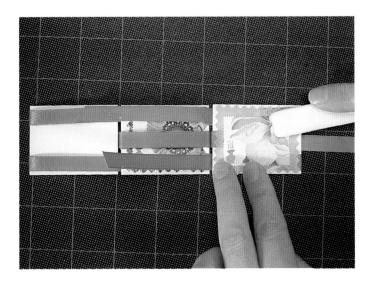

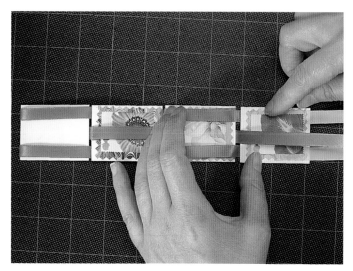

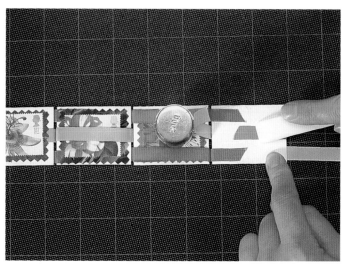

*14* Without flipping the panels over, line up the fourth panel. Fold the center ribbon from the fourth panel, which is on your left, underneath the panel. Tuck the ends of the two pink ribbons from the third panel under the left side of the fourth panel. Run the center ribbon from the third panel across the top of the fourth panel.

*15* Flip all four panels over and glue the tail ends of the two pink ribbons to the left edge of the fourth panel. Fold the end of the multicolored ribbon from the third panel over and glue on the right edge of the fourth panel.

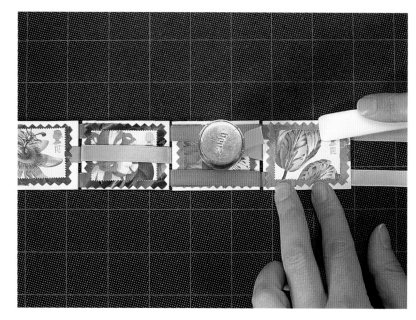

*16* Glue a bordered stamp down on top of the tails of the three ribbons. This stamp should face right side up.

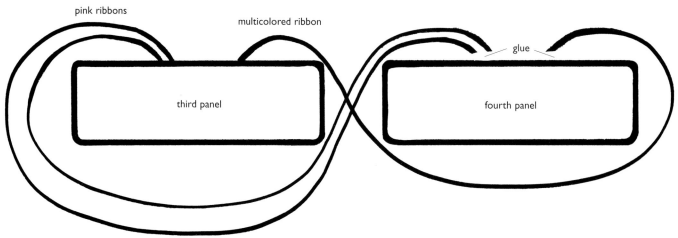

pink ribbons

multicolored ribbon

glue

third panel

fourth panel

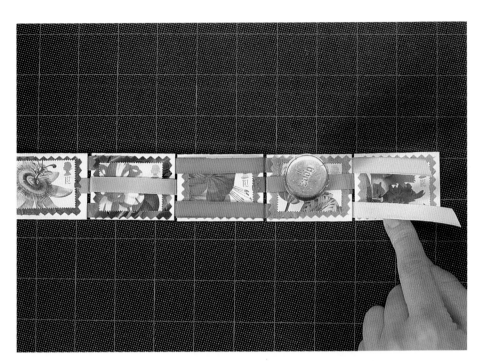

*17* Glue a bordered stamp down onto the fifth panel. Line it up so that the center ribbon from the left edge of panel four runs across panel four and tucks under the right edge of panel five. The yellow ribbons on the right of panel four will run across the top of the fifth panel.

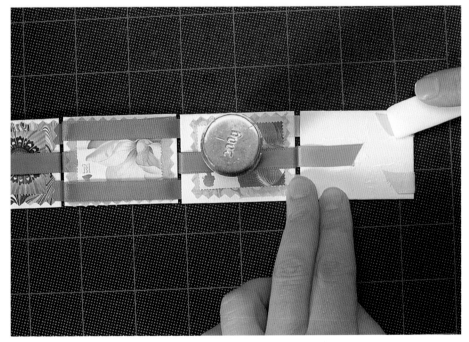

*18* Flip the entire chain over and glue the last three ribbon ends down.

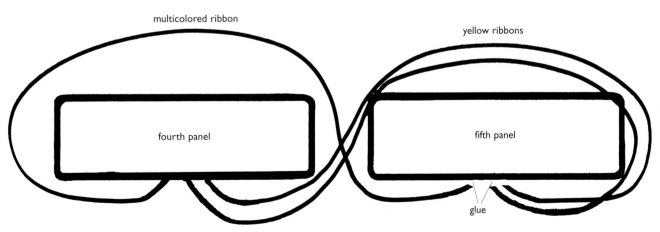

multicolored ribbon

yellow ribbons

fourth panel

fifth panel

glue

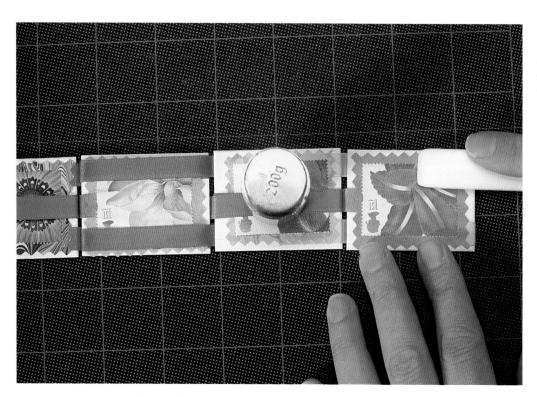

*19* Glue a bordered stamp down over the ribbon ends. The stamp should be upside down since this is the back side of the panels.

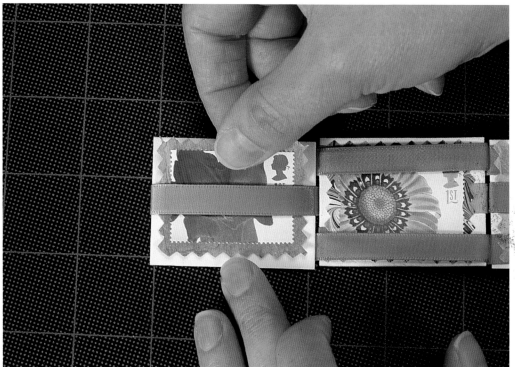

*20* Hold the first panel in your left hand and fold it under the second panel. The ladder will begin to flip along. There is now a single ribbon in the center of the first panel, which makes it easy to slide the final bordered stamp into position, if you did not do so on page 45.

# GALLERY *of* IDEAS

*Yes, Please and No, No, Never*
Emily Martin
paper, board and clear Mylar
3½" × 3½" (8.9cm × 8.9cm)

The attachments on this Jacob's ladder are invisible!

*Jabberwocky*
Maryline Poole Adams
letterpress-printed paper, wooden boards and linen tapes
2½" × 2" (6.4cm × 5.1cm)

Early click tablets were made with wooden boards that made a "click, click" sound when they fell down in order.

*Jacob's Ladder*
Susan Naylor
colored and decorated paper, board and ribbons
1⅞" × 2⅜" (4.8cm × 6cm); extends to 17¼" (43.8cm)

Color and fun and anything you'd like—these Jacob's ladders would make wonderful Valentine's gifts.

# STAR

*T*his structure is named for its shape—when fully opened so that the outside of the covers meet, it looks like a star. It is also sometimes referred to as a carousel because the pages go around and around without a beginning or end when fully opened.

This accordion book can be a single sheet, or multiple layers can be built up to create pictures or scenes.

This star is built with two accordion folds which have been placed inside a case made in the style of a hardback book cover. The case, or cover, holds the accordions together.

You can also make this book with single covered boards at the front and back and leave the accordion book free at the front and the back. You can sew through the fronts of each peak of the accordion in order to hold the various layers together.

You will want to put ties at the front and the back if you don't cover the spine. This open star can be double-sided, with scenes both on the front and back.

## WHAT YOU'LL NEED

- One sheet of handmade paper. I'm using half of a 18" × 24" (45.7cm × 61cm) sheet of Blue Jean from Cave Paper. The piece I am using is approximately 9" × 24" (22.9cm × 60.9cm).

- one piece of bright golden paper which is the same size as the blue handmade paper and about 140 lb. (300gsm) or a bit lighter in weight

- marbled paper measuring approximately 9" × 10" (22.9cm × 25.4cm) for the covering material and the inside spine

- four-ply board (or two pieces of board which are ⅟₁₆-inch to ⅛-inch thick) approximately 4⅝" × 3" (11.8cm × 7.6cm) each

- pieces of ribbon ⅜" wide × approximately 14" long (1cm × 35.6cm)

- bone folder

- card or paper to make the star patterns

- chisel or bodkin to make the ribbon hole

- cutting mat

- flat paper knife

- four pieces of blotting paper all a bit larger than the boards

- heavy craft knife

- pencil

- PVA glue, brush and container

- rough piece of board to place underneath case when punching ribbon holes

- scissors

- scrap paper

- small craft knife

- small triangle

- spring dividers

- straightedge

- strips of paper or ruler for measuring

*1* Fold the blue sheet of paper in half lengthwise. Hold the paper firmly in place with one hand and rub down the fold with the flat end of the bone folder.

*2* Position the folded edge of the paper so that it is nearest to you. Hold the paper knife or bone folder so that the flat side is flat against the work surface and near the edge. This makes it less likely to tip up while you are cutting against the fold of the paper. Slowly cut along the fold, letting the knife or bone folder find the crease in the paper. Let the knife or bone folder do the work; don't force your way through. Don't be discouraged if the first cut you make is jagged. This method of cutting paper takes some practice.

*3* Take one of the two pieces you just cut and fold it in half widthwise.

*4* Fold the top flap back on itself to meet the center fold on your right.

*5* Flip the paper over and fold the remaining flap back on itself to meet the center fold on your right.

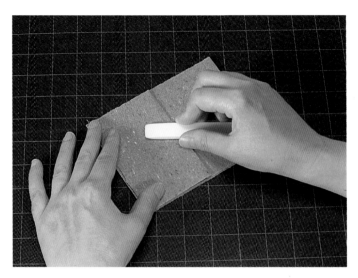

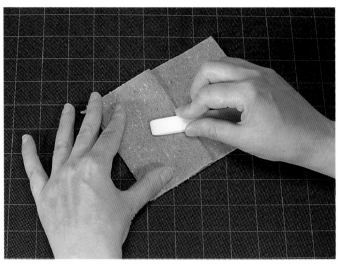

*6* Fold the new top flap back on itself to meet up with the fold you just made on your left.

*7* Flip the paper over and fold this top flap back to meet up with the fold on your left.

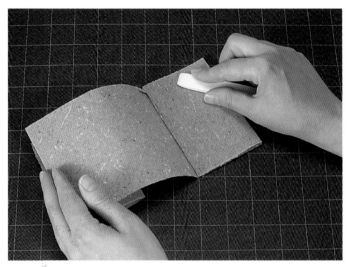

*8* Open the sheet to the center and lay on the work surface so that the center fold is a valley. Fold the righthand folds to the center to meet up on the middle crease.

*9* Fold the left set of folds to meet up with the center crease as well.

*10* This process gives you a four pointed star. (The two flaps I'm holding here that attach to the cover combine to make one point.) The easiest way to make this a five pointed star (four peaks and the two flaps attached to the cover making the fifth) is to add on the extra length.

*11* The other half of the paper you cut in step two is already the same height as the accordion you have just folded. Remember to cut the edge first to be certain you are working from a square corner or right angle. Mark and fold back a tab of about ½ inch (1.3cm).

*12* Place the strip of paper down on your work surface so that the ½-inch (1.3cm) tab is underneath on your left. Use the accordion you have already folded to mark the width of the fold you will make on the second piece of paper.

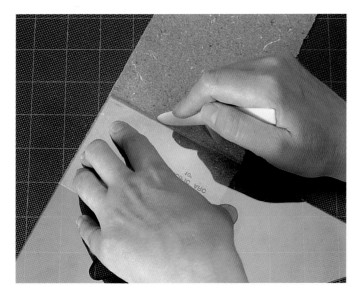

*13* Line up a plastic triangle at the edge of the paper and against the mark you have just made and score the paper along the edge of the plastic triangle. Keep your hand firmly on the triangle and fold the paper up, from behind, against the triangle's edge with the help of the bone folder.

*Hint*

*Steps eleven through eighteen explain how to make an accordion longer.*

*14* Make the next mark using the fold you have just made as a guide.

*15* Cut the paper on this mark using a plastic triangle and small knife.

*16* Check to see the pieces will match up as you would like and place them on the work surface so that there is no confusion once you have started gluing. Brush glue along the small tab.

extension tab    edge of accordion

*17* Line the folded edge of the glue-covered tab up with the edge of one end of the first accordion. Glue the tab to the underneath side of the accordion edge.

*18* Rub down the join gently with a bone folder. If the paper begins to show marks, place a clean piece of scrap paper between the bone folder and accordion to help reduce marks in the damp paper.

*19* Mark the height for the front, yellow accordion using the blue accordion as a guide.

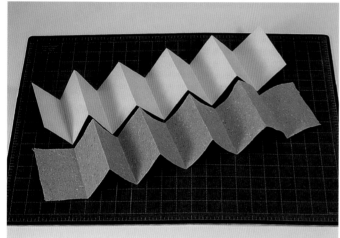

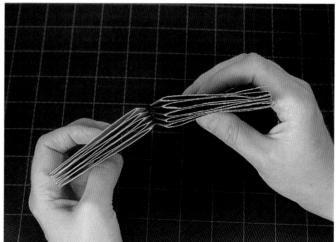

*20* Cut and fold a yellow paper accordion identical to the first blue accordion you have already assembled.

*21* Draw and cut out stars of various sizes from lightweight card. These will make drawing the pattern of stars on the yellow paper easier.

*22* Trace the outline of the stars on the back of the yellow paper. Only trace the top half of the pattern—you are creating a horizon of star shapes.

23 Cut out the pattern you have drawn with scissors or a small knife. It is often easier to keep the lines straight if you use a small triangle or straightedge to cut against.

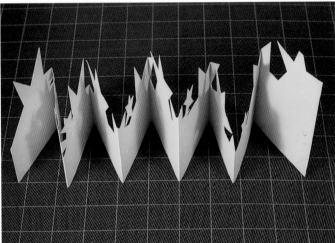

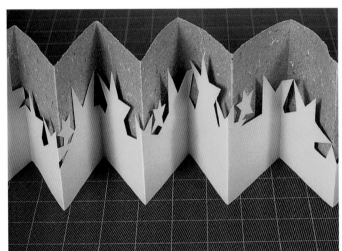

24 Once you have finished cutting the star pattern on the yellow paper, place it against the blue background and line up the folds so they fit together.

25 After you have checked that the grain of the board will go from the head to the tail of the book, measure the boards for the book by lining the book up against a right angle of the board. Place the book down on the board so that the spine of the book is hanging out and over the edge of the board by about ⅛ inch (0.3cm). Mark the board so the cover will have an equal square at the head, tail and foredge.

*26* Cut a front and back board. A plastic triangle will help to keep the angles straight and a heavy craft knife is needed to cut through the board safely.

*27* Hold the book between the boards so that the boards are positioned where you will want them to be when you make the case to cover the book. This means that you will be able to see approximately ⅛ inch (0.3cm) of the book pages at the spine.

*28* Holding the book in place with one hand, mark from one board edge to the other board edge using a scrap of paper. If things won't stay in place, measure the spine width of the book and add ¼ inch (0.6cm) in order to arrive at the measurement. If you use very heavy boards, you must add a little more space for the covering material to travel up and over that edge.

*29* Transfer this measurement to the spring dividers.

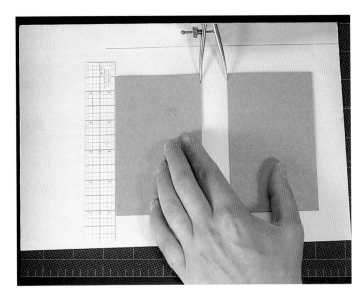

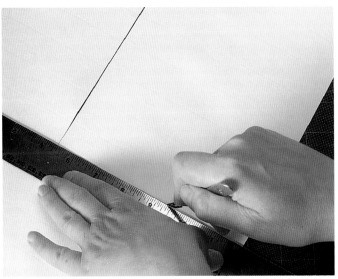

*30* Mark the wrong side or inside of the covering material (the marbled paper in this case). Place the boards down with a 1-inch (2.5cm) margin all around and the spine measurement (the spine of the book + approximately ¼ inch) in the middle between the boards. Keep the grain going head to tail.

*31* Cut out the piece of paper you have measured.

*32* Cut out a piece of cloth and a piece of marbled paper which will be used to line the spine. Make the cloth piece the same height as the boards you cut in step 26 and the width of the spine plus 2 inches (5.1cm); this will create an overlap of 1 inch (2.5cm) on either side. Cut the paper piece to the height of the book and the width of the spine plus 2 inches (5.1cm). Trim off all four corners of both pieces.

*33* Nip off the corners of the boards. Check to see there are no rough edges and everything is ready to be glued together. Draw guidelines if you feel it will make it easier. I always draw the top margin line in pencil across the cover material (see the next step). You have now assembled all the materials you will need to begin gluing. Position all the pieces and tools so they are within easy reach. Place a sheet of waste paper on the workbench and begin to brush the glue onto one board with a stippling motion; this will help you distribute the glue evenly.

*34* Position the board down on the reverse side of the covering material. Working from left to right you will have a border of approximately 1 inch (2.5cm) extra covering material at the left and above and below the board. Once it is in position, press down firmly with both hands flat on top of the board.

*35* Flip the entire piece over. Place clean scrap paper over the cover and use a bone folder to gently rub the covering material down to be certain there are no air pockets between the board and covering material.

*36* Flip the cover back to the reverse side and use your set spring dividers to mark the space between the two boards.

*37* Glue the second board and position it as you did the first.

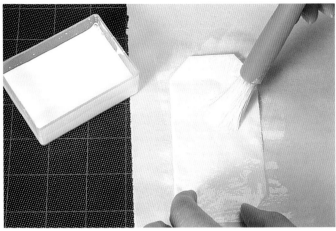

*38* Glue the spine cloth using a brushing stroke. Always throw scrap paper away once you have used it—you don't want to accidentally lay your book on glue-covered paper.

*39* Position the spine cloth so it is centered and rub it down gently with the bone folder so that it fits neatly in between the boards.

*40* Hold two strips of scrap board against the corner edges of the cover board to measure miter cuts for the cover paper corners. Miter all four corners of the cover paper in this way. This extra paper at the corners will allow the covering material to wrap over the tips of the board corners when you fold in the covering material.

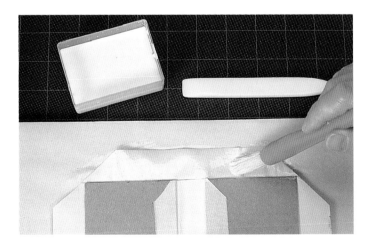

*41* Glue the head covering material.

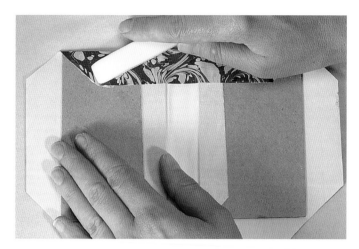

*42* Pull the covering material up and over the edge before you rub it down flat on the inside of the board. Be careful while the material is damp with glue, but remember this is one place where air often gets trapped. Work with the bone folder and your fingers and hands.

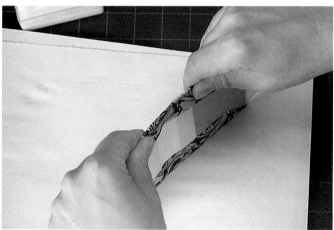

*43* Glue and turn in the tail covering material next.

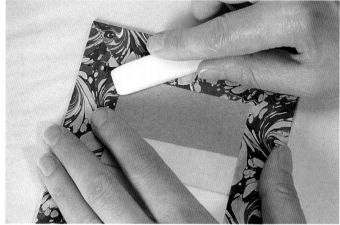

*44* Apply glue to the covering material on one foredge. Nip in the material over the very tip of the corner using either your fingers or a bone folder.

*45* Fold the material over and rub it down gently.

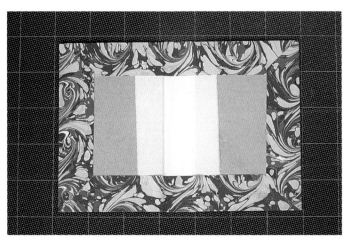

*46* Glue and fold in the other foredge.

*47* Glue and position the center covering piece. Rub it down gently so that it fits in snugly between the two boards.

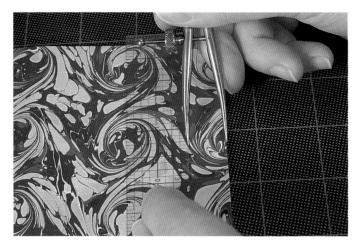

*48* Mark the position of the ribbons. These are about a ½-inch (1.3cm) from the board edge and just above the halfway point of the height of the boards.

*49* Punch a hole with a chisel or awl. Use a piece of scrap board underneath if you are working on a cutting mat; you may dig a hole in the mat if you work directly on it.

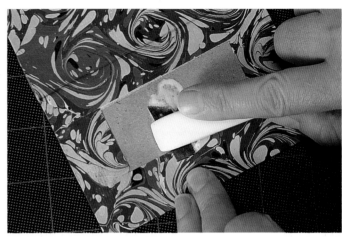

*50* Pull the ribbon through the hole from the front. Leave a piece about ½ inch (1.3cm) long inside the cover. A point at the end of the dividers or one end of a metal triangle can be used to push the ribbon through if it won't slide in easily.

*51* Glue the ribbon down on the inside of the case and rub it flat with a bone folder.

*52* Glue down the last back panel of the blue background accordion onto the back board of the book case.

*53* Glue, position and press down the top layer of stars.

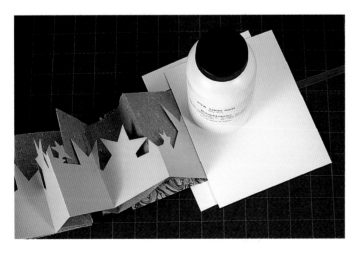

*54* Place the back board with the two panels attached between two pieces of blotting paper, like a sandwich. Put a light weight on top and let it dry for half an hour or so before attaching the front of the accordion to the front board.

# GALLERY *of* IDEAS

### *The King's Breakfast*
Maryline Poole Adams
letterpress printed paper, board and velvet ribbon
2⅞" × 1¾₆" (7.3cm × 5cm)

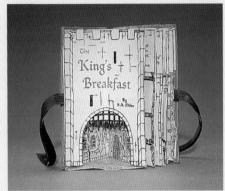

Room after room
and scene after scene,
this story unfolds
with the text running
all along the turret.
This miniature book
is full of new detail
and discoveries each
time you look
through it.

### *1996 Miniature Book Conclave–San Francisco*
designed and illustrated by Dianne Ewell Weiss
cloth-covered boards and spine, color and black-and-white
copied art, ribbon
9¼" × 6⅞" × 1" (23.5cm × 17.5cm × 2.5cm)

These scenes of San
Francisco were the
centerpieces at the
Miniature Book
Conclave's banquet
dinner in 1996.
Extra copies were
sold to those people
not lucky enough to
win the star book at
their table.

# SINGLE SECTION PAMPHLET

Traditionally, one sheet of paper folded and cut makes a single section. If the sheet is folded once it is a folio section with two leaves of paper; folded twice it is a quarto with four leaves of paper; folded three times it becomes an octavo with eight leaves and folded four times a sexto–decimo with sixteen leaves. Because the leaves all come from a single sheet of paper, all of the above examples are considered single sections.

The term single section refers to the paper inside the book. When a cover or wrapper is attached, it becomes a pamphlet.

This is one of the simplest ways of putting pages together and has often been used for short religious and political publications.

The most common single section pamphlet we see now is a magazine stapled through the middle.

In the English binding trade, up until about the middle of the 1900s, one of the largest sheets of paper available for books measured 28" × 23" (71.1cm × 58.4cm). This sheet was called an "elephant." Therefore, one of the largest books you can find in a rare book library will be called an "elephant folio," which is approximately 23" × 14" (58.4cm × 35.6cm).

## WHAT YOU'LL NEED

- Four to six sheets of 8½" × 11" (21.6cm × 27.9cm) stationery paper, whose grain runs head to tail when it is folded in half to 8½" high × 5½" wide (21.6cm × 14cm). I'm using Crane Premium Presentation Paper, Resume, which is 32 lb. (70gsm) and 100 percent cotton fiber. It comes in boxes of 50 and 500 sheets. The color I'm using is Ecruwhite.

- A heavier piece of paper—something about 140 lb. (300gsm)—which is just over 8½" (21.6cm) high × 14" (35.6cm) to 16½" (41.9cm) wide. I'm using Taxicab Yellow in Light Art Weight from Twinrocker.

- bone folder
- cutting mat
- large triangle
- needle
- pencil
- ruler or scraps of paper for measuring
- scissors
- small craft knife
- straightedge
- waxed thread

*1* Fold each sheet of paper in half. Line up the top corners and free edges. Using the flat end of your bone folder, gently rub down the fold. Fold as many sheets of paper as you would like for your section and place them inside one another to form a single section.

*2* Place your section flat and approximately ⅛ inch (0.3cm) from the tail edge of your cover paper. Mark the same distance from the head of the pages onto the cover paper with a pencil.

*3* Transfer the measurement you have just made onto a strip of scrap paper.

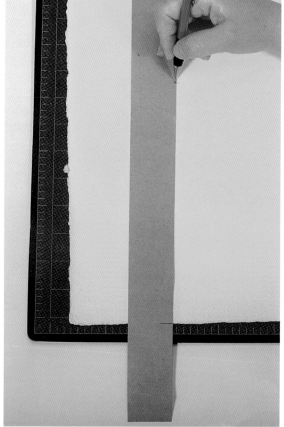

*4* You can now use the measurement on the strip of paper to mark the same measurement in several places along the length of your cover paper in order to cut the sheet equally all along.

*5* Place your straightedge along the measurements. Hold the straightedge firmly in place with one hand and cut the cover paper with a scalpel or craft knife.

*6* The width of your cover paper should be about 2½ times the width of your book. You can cut this down more precisely after you've sewn the section into the cover. You can make a softer edge, similar to a deckle in handmade paper, by first scoring the paper with a bone folder and then tearing the paper by pulling it against a triangle or straightedge.

*7* Measure and cut one piece of thread approximately three times the height of your book.

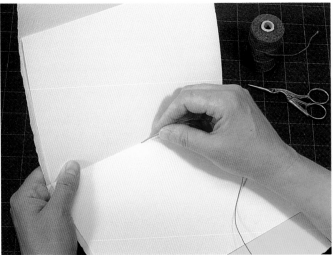

*8* Thread your needle. Fold your cover paper in half and position the section of pages inside the cover. Begin sewing by pushing the needle through the center from the inside.

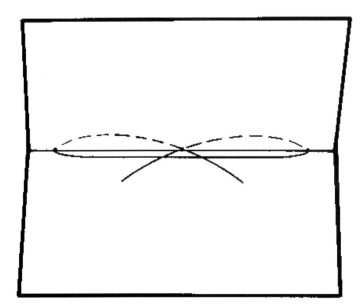

sewing diagram

*9* Pull the needle through the center of the cover on the outside.

*10* It is easier to punch holes through the fold from the inside. Bring your needle around from the outside and punch a hole approximately ½ inch (1.3cm) in from the edge of the cover, but don't sew through this way. Return your threaded needle back to the outside of the cover.

*11* From the outside, push your needle through the hole you just made and pull it through to the inside.

*12* Carry the thread along to the opposite end of the book and punch another hole approximately ½ inch (1.3cm) from the edge of the cover. Push the needle through to the outside.

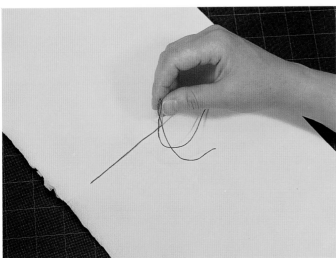

*13* From the outside, push the needle through the center hole again, being careful not to get your needle caught in the thread already there.

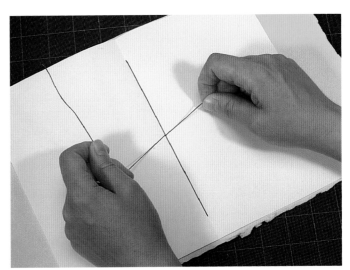

*14* Hold a thread end in each hand on either side of the center thread and pull gently to tighten.

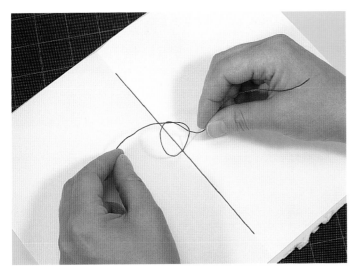

*15* Loop the righthand thread over the left and then the lefthand thread over the right to tie a square knot. Pull the threads tight.

*16* Cut the threads so they are long enough to retie if they should come undone.

*17* Now you can measure the foredge or front edge of the cover. This distance should be the same as the square at the head and tail of the cover.

*18* Score the edge with a bone folder against a triangle which is lined up with the head of the cover.

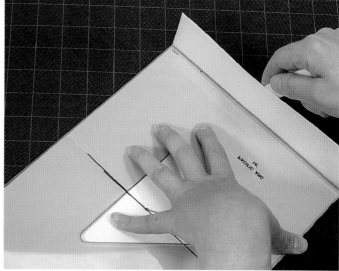

*19* Fold the flap up against the right angle. Trim the edge if you want the front and back flaps to be even in width.

# GALLERY *of* IDEAS

### *Spider Poems*
bindings by Carolyn Whitesel; text by Jeff Worley
letterpress printed at Larkspur Press
9⅜" × 5¾" (23.8cm × 14.6cm)

Four variations of this pamphlet-sewn booklet are slipcased into paper covers decorated with eraser and foam stamps and pencil lines.

### *Woods Story*
John Cutrone; binding by
Gabrielle Fox
twig, leather and thread
2⅞" × 3⅛" (7.3cm × 7.9cm)

Twist the thread around a pencil or straw as I have done around this twig. Wrap the thread around as you are sewing and it will be held in place as you sew through the cover.

# DOUBLE SECTION PAMPHLET

This is the simplest way to make a sewn book which has just a few more pages than the previous book. The sewing is a little stronger because the pages and cover are anchored with thread going through a few more holes. The extra holes can be used for taller single sections as well. You can even add additional holes, but not so many that the spine becomes perforated with holes too close together!

You can use the pleat in the middle as a division for two books and start a different book at each end. It's fun to begin one book going one way and then flip the book over and begin the other book upside down.

## WHAT YOU'LL NEED

- Eight to twelve sheets of 8½" × 11" (21.6cm × 27.9cm) stationery paper, whose grain runs head to tail when it is folded in half to 8½" high × 5½" wide (21.6cm × 14cm). I'm using Crane Premium Presentation Paper, Resume, which is 32 lb. (70gsm) and 100 percent cotton fiber. It comes in boxes of 50 and 500 sheets. The color I'm using is Ecruwhite.

- A heavier piece of paper—something about 140 lb. (300gsm)—which is just over 8½" (21.6cm) high × 16½" (41.9cm) wide. I'm using Double X in Light Art Weight from Twinrocker.

- two bull dog clips

- beeswax

- colored linen thread

- cutting mat

- large triangle

- needle

- pencil

- ruler or strips of paper for measuring

- scissors

- spring dividers

- straightedge

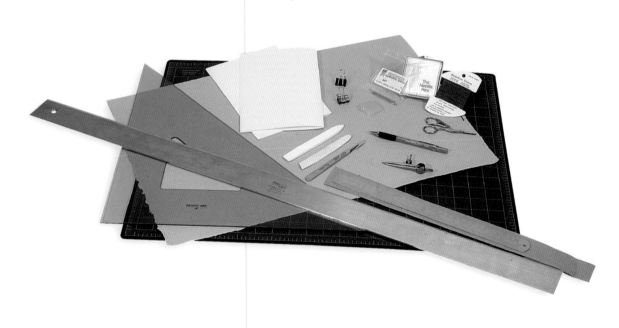

*1* Cut a straight edge across the top of the wrapper paper before you do anything else. Position one section of paper on the cover paper and mark the square you would like for the cover.

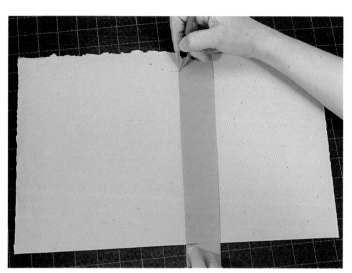

*2* Transfer this measurement to a scrap of paper and use this guide to mark the height of the cover in several places along the length of the cover.

*3* Place your straightedge up against the marks and cut the edge of the cover with a small craft knife or scalpel.

*4* Fold the cover in half widthwise.

*5* Measure a ½ inch (1.3cm) with a pair of spring dividers or a scrap of paper.

*6* Transfer that measurement to the front and back sides of the cover, measuring from the folded edge.

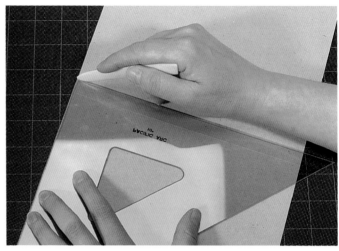

*7* Open the cover and lay it flat in order to score each side of the center pleat separately. Using a right angle and bone folder, score the fold.

*8* Then push the fold against the plastic triangle from the back.

*9* You now have a center pleat. Fold the cover in half with the peak of the center fold facing you as I have done here.

*10* Use bull dog clips to keep the two sections in position on the cover as you punch holes and sew up the book.

*11* Position a section on each side of the center fold or peak so that the center fold of the section lines up with the fold or valley on each side of the cover.

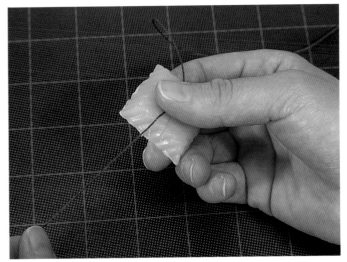

*12* Measure and cut a piece of thread which is approximately three times the height of the book.

*13* Pull the thread lightly against the beeswax. Waxing thread makes it a bit more manageable and less likely to tear paper. It also gives more grip when tying knots. When you have waxed the whole length, thread a needle.

*14* You will find it easier to punch the holes while you are sewing up the book because the holes you have already threaded help to keep the sections and cover in position. Begin sewing through the center from the inside of one section through the two folds or valley of the cover and out again through the center of the second section.

*15* There are five holes to be made and sewn through. The second hole is halfway between the center hole and the edge hole, which is approximately ½ inch (1.3cm) from the edge of the section, as shown earlier in the single section sewing steps. Flip the book over and come back through hole number two.

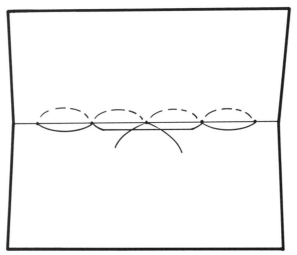

sewing diagram

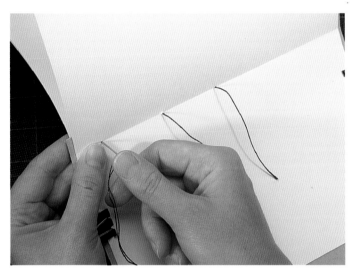

*16* Take the thread down to the end and go out through the end hole.

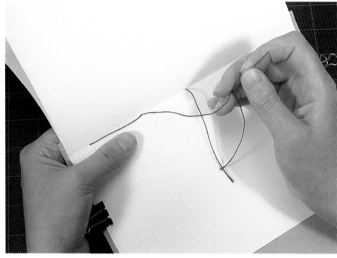

*17* Loop back up and through hole number two again, coming back in toward the center where you started.

*18* Pull the thread past the center hole and go out through the next hole, which is centered between the hole at the edge of the paper and the hole in the center.

*19* Punch the last hole approximately ½ inch (1.3cm) from the edge of the book.

*20* Bring the thread through from the back and pull it to the second hole in from the edge. Push the needle out to the back again.

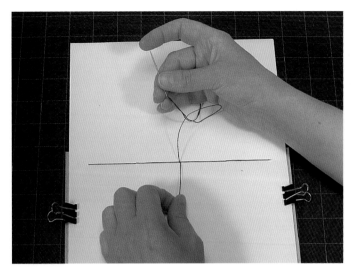

*21* Working from the back, bring the thread through the center hole to the front, being careful not to get caught up in the thread already here.

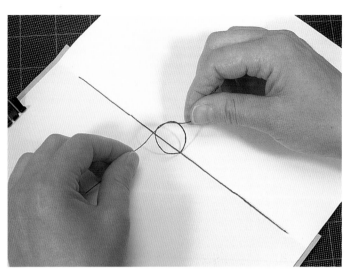

*22* Pull the threads tight—but not so tight that you distort the paper—and make a square knot with the center thread running through in the middle. Cross the right thread over the left. Then cross the left thread over the right and pull to secure the knot. Trim off the tails.

*23* Use spring dividers or a scrap of paper to take the measurement of the square of the cover.

*24* Transfer that measurement to the foredge of each side of the cover.

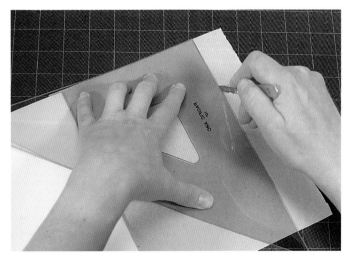

*25* Line up a plastic triangle at the top edge of the cover and at the mark you have just made and cut along the edge with a small craft knife or scalpel.

# GALLERY *of* IDEAS

## Zootaxy
Charles Alexander; illustration by Cynthia Miller
letterpress-printed text with colored paper covers
6¾" × 6¾" (17.2cm × 17.2cm)

The brown and red cover papers are sewn in together. The
red paper slots through a cut slit in the front and back of
the brown paper wrapper.

## Hawaiian Scroll
Hedi Kyle
painted corrugated
paper, rolled and
woven yellow pad
sheets painted with
methyl cellulose and
graphite, burned
marks
9¼" × 3"
(23.5cm × 7.6cm)

This may have been
made with the inside
pleat on the outside.
If you make a similar
structure, remember
that the center sheets
facing you will be the
sheet of paper which
makes the pleat.

# MULTI-SECTION PAMPHLET

**M**any materials were used as surfaces for communication during and after the widespread use of papyrus, such as palm leaves, metals, wood, tree bark, parchment (sheep or goat skin), vellum (lamb, kid or calf skin) and woven cloth. None of these is as versatile or can be made to fulfill as many different and specific uses as handmade paper. Handmade paper possesses characteristics and qualities which are different in each sheet you handle.

The first known use of paper was in the second century B.C. in China. The process of making a formed, dried sheet of paper from pulp or fibers suspended in water was a closely-guarded secret. It wasn't until the twelfth century that it reached Europe; the influence of the Moors spread its use from Spain through Northern Africa.

By the fifteenth century paper was being made in England, and in the seventeenth century paper making was brought to Pennsylvania by German settlers.

Paper can be made from many different fibers; each has its own characteristics. The paper I used for the pages of this book is made of cotton fiber. Flower petals were floated in the pulp causing them to imbed in the sheet of paper. Other decorated, handmade papers might have flowers or threads pressed into the sheet after it has been formed, but before it has dried.

## WHAT YOU'LL NEED

- One 25¼" × 19¾" (64.1cm × 50.2cm) sheet of handmade paper with flower inclusions which is text weight. Mine is from La Papeterie Saint-Gilles, Canada. You will fold and cut this sheet into pages.

- A heavier piece of paper for the cover—something about 140 lb. (300gsm). This cover will be stronger if you use handmade paper. You need a sheet 8½" (21.6cm) high × 16½" (41.9cm) to 19¼" (48.9cm) wide. I'm using Lavender Light in Art Weight from Twinrocker.

- one piece of paper or card which is the same height as the pages and about 4 inches wide (10.2cm)

- beeswax

- bodkin or needle to punch holes

- bone folder

- card for making a spine template

- cutting mat

- linen thread in two colors

- needle

- pencil

- scissors

- small craft knife

- small weight

- spring dividers

- straightedge

- strips of paper or ruler for measuring

*1* Making sheets and folds of paper for a book from a larger sheet can be done by folding the sheet of paper over and over and cutting at each fold in order to easily get final sheets that are all the same size. Begin by folding the sheet of paper in half so that it is half the length it was originally. Remember to hold the paper in place with one hand and crease the fold with a bone folder in the other hand.

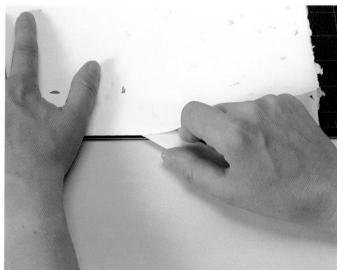

*2* Deckle-edged paper can be more attractive if the paper is cut with a bone folder in order to give a softer, less defined edge. It can be difficult to get the cut started, so use a knife to just begin the tearing of the paper. A bone folder can then be used to complete the cut. Lay the flat side of the bone folder against the work surface and place the fold you are cutting near the edge of the work surface. This will help you avoid tipping up the bone folder, which can give you a more irregular edge than you are trying to achieve. Let the bone folder do the work, pulling it against the fold little by little.

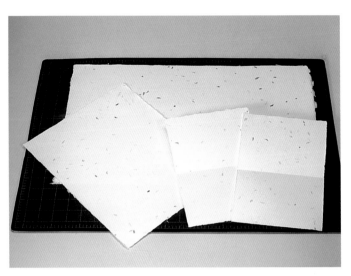

*3* Continue to fold and cut the paper in half until you have sheets the size you desire.

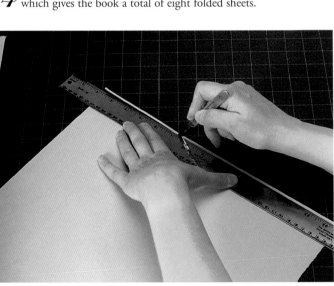

*4* This project is made up of four sets of two folded sheets each, which gives the book a total of eight folded sheets.

*5* Measure the height of the book wrapper by marking a little over the height of the pages. An ⅛ of an inch (0.3cm) at the head and tail is the most that will work well with a soft wrapper. If you have a larger square or border, the paper tends to get squashed over and wears badly.

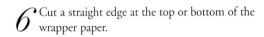

*6* Cut a straight edge at the top or bottom of the wrapper paper.

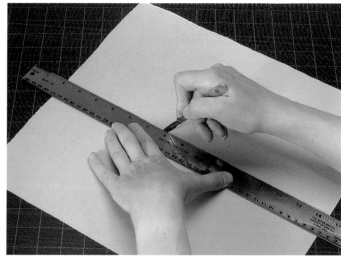

*7* Transfer the measurement for the height of the wrapper to the cover paper and cut it using a straightedge and small craft knife.

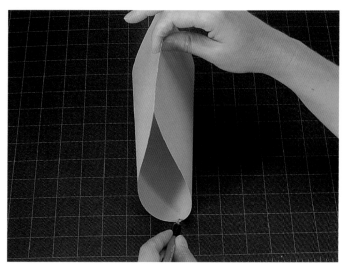

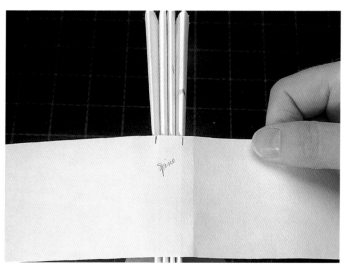

*8* Gently fold the wrapper in half lengthwise and lightly mark the center point in pencil.

*9* Measure the thickness or depth of the book. Hold the sections so there is a little spring, not pressed flat. This allows for the thickness of the thread when taking this measurement.

*10* Transfer the measurement from step nine to the center point of the wrapper so that the new marks are on either side of the center point you previously marked. Erase the center mark.

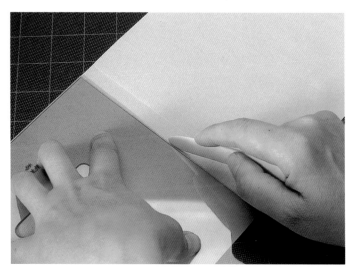
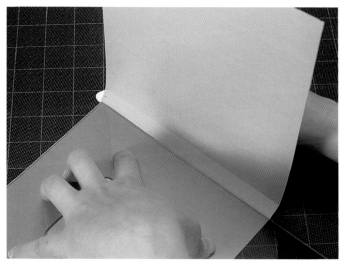

*11* Score and fold the paper at these two marks. This will create a spine in the wrapper.

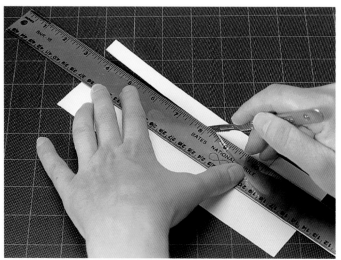

*12* Measuring an exact template of the spine will make the next few steps more manageable. Cut the template from a piece of light card.

*13* The sewing pattern for the book is worked out first on the template. The holes to be sewn through can then be transferred from the template to the spine of the wrapper. There are four sections in this book, so four lengthwise sets of holes will be needed to sew all four sections into the cover. Each section is sewn into the wrapper individually, as if it was a single section or pamphlet. Imagine the spine of the wrapper and think where you would like the lines of thread to run. Avoid too many holes right next to one another because it will make a perforated line and tear easily. Measuring from head to tail, draw straight lines across the template in the positions where you would like to place the holes.

*14* Now divide the width of the template into fifths, making the first and last fifths a tiny bit wider to allow for the wrapper folding over with a flap inside. It is a minute measurement, but it does allow the covers to sit more comfortably. This is much easier to do with spring dividers. Each section needs to be secure in the wrapper. Some sections will hold with only two holes—one near the head and one near the tail. Other sections can be sewn in with three holes or more. The first and last sections of this book are sewn in with three holes lengthwise, as you would sew a traditional pamphlet or single section. The holes are positioned in the same places for both of these sections. The two middle sections are sewn in with two holes—one near the head and one near the tail. They too have holes in the same positions. Mark the position of the holes at the intersections of the two sets of lines as shown below.

1. Mark lines for position of four sets of holes from head to tail.

3. Mark holes at intersections of the two lines as shown.

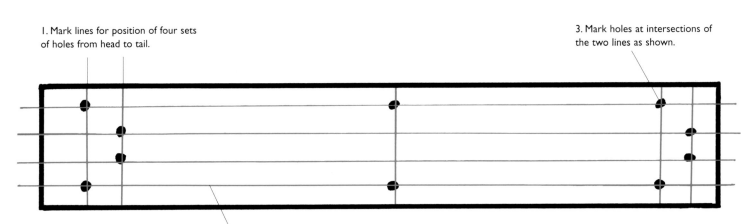

2. Divide width into fifths, making first and last fifth minutely wider.

*15* Position the template over the outside of the spine of the wrapper and use a bodkin or needle to punch the marked holes into the cover.

*16* Position the sections in the wrapper to see where you would like the sections to be placed from head to tail and how the borders or squares of the wrapper will appear once the pages are sewn into the cover.

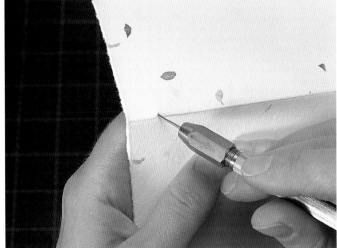

*17* Open the wrapper and line up each section. Mark the holes from the spine onto the sections with a pencil, then punch the holes with a bodkin or needle.

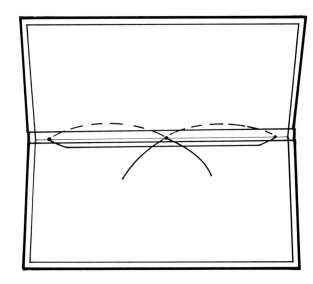

sewing diagram for first and fourth sections

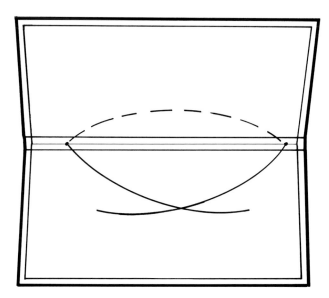

sewing diagram for
second and third
sections

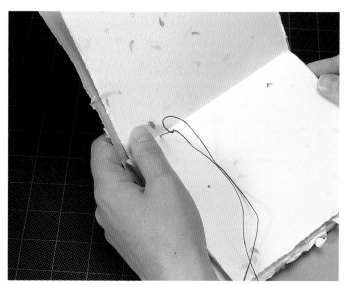

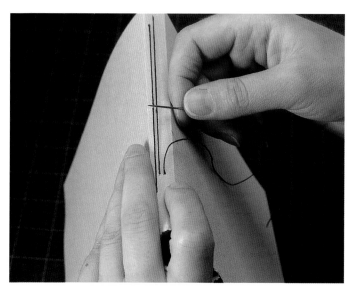

*18* The sections can be sewn into the wrapper in any order. I've already sewn in the first two sections so that you can see
the lines of thread along the spine of the wrapper making up the pattern. The third section, just as the second, is sewn
using two holes. Cut a length of thread which is three times the height of the book. Wax the thread if it isn't already waxed
and thread the needle. Push the needle through from the inside to the outside of the wrapper using one of the end holes.

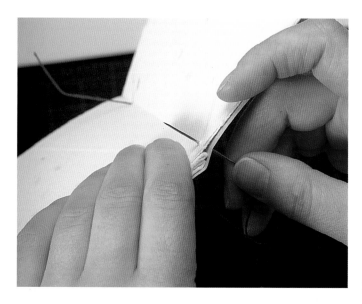

*19* Carry the thread along the outside of
the spine to the other end hole and
push back through to the inside of the section.

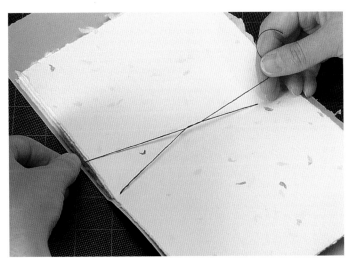

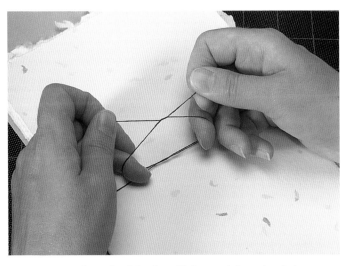

*20* To tie a square knot, cross the ends of the thread right over left. If it feels difficult to manage, cross it right over left again.

*21* Cross the ends of the thread left over right and pull the threads tight. Snip off the ends. Always leave enough thread to retie if for some reason the knot should come undone or you would like to untie it.

*22* The first and last sections are sewn in as single sections with three holes. Cut a piece of thread three times the height of the book, wax it and thread the needle. Begin with the center hole and push the needle through from the inside pages to the outside of the wrapper. Leave a tail of at least 3 inches (7.6cm) inside the section.

*23* Take the thread, on the outside, up to the hole at either the head or tail and go back into the section of pages.

*24* Run the thread along inside the section from one end to the other and go out again at the hole at the other end.

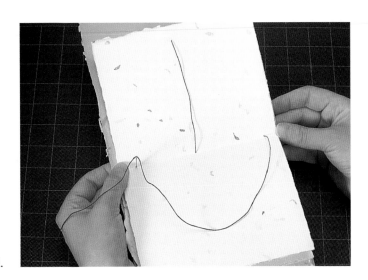

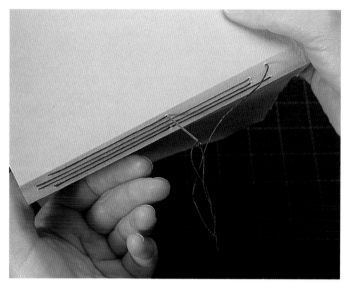

*25* From the outside wrapper, push the needle back in through the center hole. Be careful not to catch the needle in the thread already there because it will make pulling the thread tight to knot it difficult.

*26* Tie a square knot as shown for sections two and three and snip the ends of the threads.

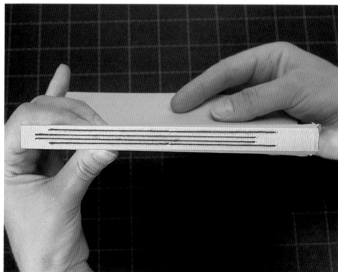

*27* Mark and score flaps for the front and back covers or cut the wrapper paper equally at front and back.

The finished spine.

# GALLERY *of* IDEAS

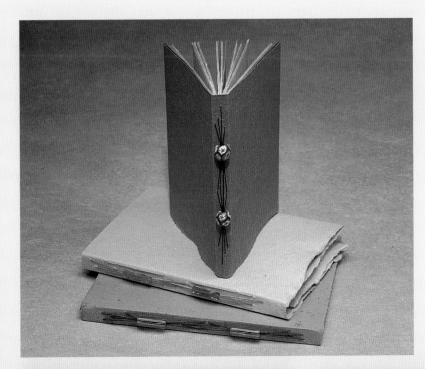

### *Two Beads*
Marianne Rogenski
handmade paper, thread and beads
6" × 4" (15.2 × 10.2cm)

The standing book displays how stunning the simple pattern of sewing can become with this choice of colors.

### *Untitled Blank Book*
Eric Alstrom
cast paper cover, paper and thread
6¼" × 4½" (15.9cm × 11.4cm)

Wrappers or covers can be made of nearly anything as long as the material will flex at the joint so you can open and shut the book.

### *Erté Maquettes*
Rebecca Saady Bingham; binding by Gabrielle Fox
printed text, leather, card, colored tissue and thread
2⅞" × 2¼" (7.3cm × 5.7cm)

A separate gray spine piece has been sewn on at the same time the book was sewn into the leather wrapper. Wood, buttons or shaped pieces of card can also be used to decorate and reinforce the spine. Remember though that if the spine pieces are stiff, the book won't flex wide open.

June 15, 1981

Today was the first day I
woke and knew you were
there. I wonder if you are a
boy or a girl and what you
will look like. How wonderful
it will be for you to read
this journal when you are

# BUTTERFLY WITH FOLDED WRAPPER

his Japanese style of binding is widely known as four-needle sewing or butterfly. There are other Japanese styles of binding which are four hole, but not sewn with four needles. There is also one other style of binding known as butterfly which has all the pages stuck together at the spine. To be clear, we can call this version the sewn butterfly.

The movement and flexibility of this structure once sewn makes it ideal for notebooks and sketchbooks. It opens flat at every page, and depending on how you cover it, can be soft or made rigid with boards to support your writing or drawing.

The cover for the sewn butterfly is made of a paper wrapper just like the ones children make to protect their school books.

## WHAT YOU'LL NEED

- Sixteen sheets of 8½" × 11" (21.6cm × 27.9cm) stationery paper, whose grain runs head to tail when it is folded in half to 8½" high × 5½" wide (21.6cm × 14cm). I'm using Crane Premium Presentation Paper, Resume, which is 32 lb. (70gsm) and 100 percent cotton fiber. It comes in boxes of 50 and 500 sheets. The color I'm using is Ecruwhite.

- one 20" × 30¾" (50.8cm × 78.1cm), 70 lb. (150gsm) piece of Canford paper by Daler-Rowney in Coffee

- one piece of paper or card which is the same height as the pages and about 4 inches (10.2cm) wide

- beeswax

- bodkin or needle for punching holes

- bone folder

- cutting mat

- four needles

- large triangle

- pencil

- scissors

- small craft knife

- small weight

- straightedge

- strips of paper for measuring

- thin, strong thread

*Hint*

*The sewn butterfly makes a very good album. Cut most of every other page of this book out or cut and fold the paper with tabs before you sew the book. See the instructions in project three for help.*

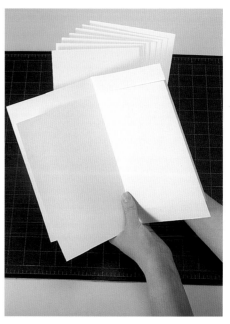

*1* Fold the sheets of paper in half. Hold the paper firmly in position with one hand and gently rub down the fold using a bone folder.

*2* Place one fold into another to form sections. This book is made up of sixteen sheets of paper folded in half. Each of the eight sections contains two folded sheets.

*3* Fold the piece of lightweight card in half. With a pencil, mark three roughly equal spaces from head to tail. Make a mark for a hole at each end which is approximately ½ inch (1.3cm) in from the edge of the paper. Position the other two marks for holes so that the sewing is spaced approximately in thirds.

sewing diagram

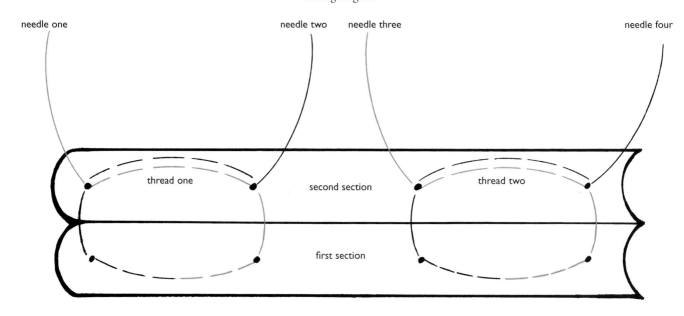

needle one        needle two    needle three        needle four

thread one    second section    thread two

first section

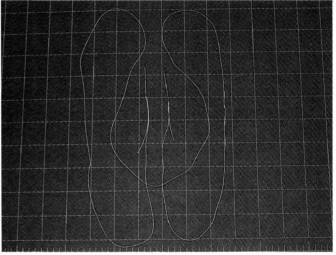

*4* Line the pattern you have just made up with the head edge of the section. Here it is lined up at the right and a light weight has been placed on top to keep the pattern in position. Punch the holes in each section, one section at a time, using the pattern and an awl or needle to make the holes.

*5* Hold a piece of thin thread up to a section of the book to measure a piece that is two-thirds the height of the book. Multiply this measurement by eight—the number of sections to be sewn. You will need two pieces of thin thread of this length.

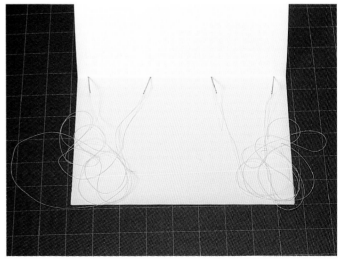

*6* Thread a needle onto each end of both pieces of thread. The four needles I used are the self threading type. Thread the needle through the bottom hole and snap the thread tail back into the top hole; the needle is unlikely to fall off. If you don't have these needles, push the needle through the thread after you have threaded it through the needle and catch the needle securely in that loop of thread. Sewing with four needles can take forever if the needles keep dropping off.

*7* Think of the needles as two pairs. Begin sewing from the inside of the first section. Push needle one through the lefthand hole near the edge of the paper. Push needle two, attached to the other end of needle one's thread, through the next hole to the right. Push needle three, on the second piece of thread, through the next hole to the right and needle four through the last hole which is close to the other end of the paper.

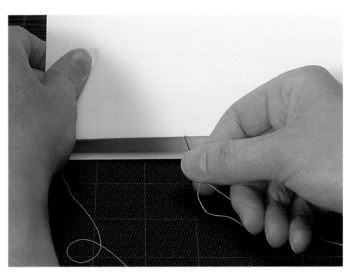

*8* Close the section and turn it so that the spine is facing you. Pull the two sets of needles through to the outside until the threads are equal in length and fairly tight against the paper. Lift up the paper and make sure that the loops are flat against the fold inside and there are no twists or knots in the thread. It is important to keep the threads straight and the tension of your sewing even as you sew the book together. It is very difficult to go back and make adjustments.

*9* Place the second section on top of the first with the holes lined up. A light weight can be placed inside the section to hold it in place.

*10* From the outside, push needle two through the second hole in the second section.

*11* Open up the section and pull needle two through the paper to the inside. Then carry it over to your left and out of the first hole. Push needle one from the outside through the first hole and then, from the inside, across and out the second hole. Repeat the same pattern for needles three and four. Work in pairs and think of the threads as your arms folding over; right hand to the left and left hand to the right. Build the book up section by section, repeating the same pattern. The needle below goes straight up to the matching hole above in the next section. Always check for twists, knots and thread tension before beginning to sew on the next section.

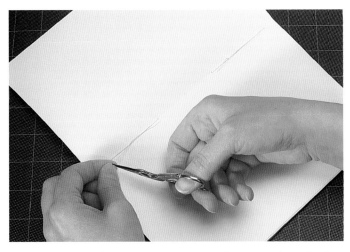

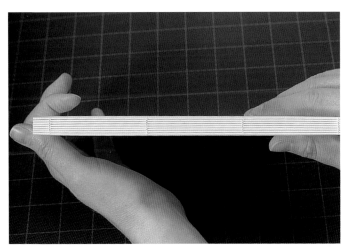

*12* Inside the final section tie two square knots. Tie the ends of the threads attached to needle one and two right over left and left over right. Repeat for the threads attached to needles three and four. Cut off the ends, but leave tails long enough to retie if the knots come undone.

*13* The sewn book should be fairly even all along the spine when closed. The thread is slightly recessed into the holes in the paper.

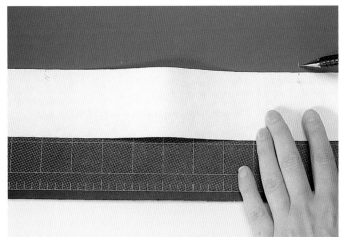

*14* You can use strips of scrap paper to mark the measurements for the paper wrapper. Measure the height of the book plus a small distance to allow the pages to slide into the cover easily when they are placed into the wrapper. An ⅛ inch (0.3cm) should be enough.

*15* Measure the width of the book and again allow an extra ⅛ inch (0.3cm) to allow for all the folded paper at the spine and foredge.

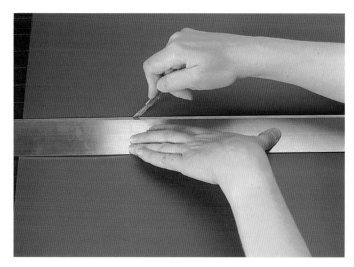

*16* Make a straight cut across the top of the cover paper with a straightedge and small craft knife or scalpel.

*17* Measure somewhere between one-third and half the height of the book. This measurement is for the flaps that fold in at the head and tail of the wrapper. If they are exactly half the height, they have a tendency to jam up when the wrapper is folded up.

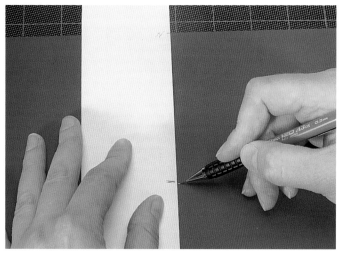

*18* Transfer that measurement to the top of the wrapper paper. Mark from the straight edge down.

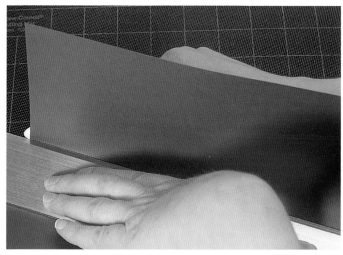

*19* Score and fold over along the marks you made for the top flap of the wrapper.

*20* Transfer the height measurement to the wrapper. Measure from the fold down. Score and fold over along the marks you have just made.

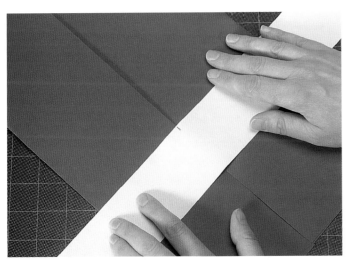

*21* The bottom flap may be too wide, so use the same measurement you used for the top flap to mark the width of the bottom flap.

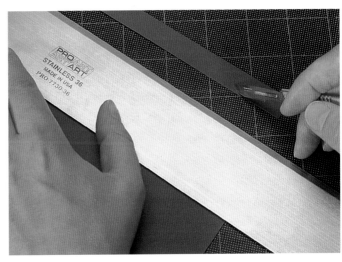

*22* Line the straightedge up along the marks and cut any extra paper off.

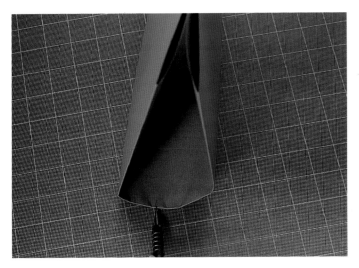

*23* Fold the wrapper gently in half widthwise. Mark the center point with a pencil.

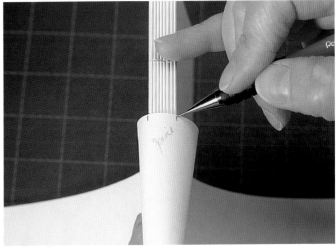

*24* Measure the width of the spine at the widest point. The book will be wider in the areas where there is a double thread used for sewing. Don't make this measurement too tight. If you use a very heavy paper for the wrapper, remember that at the spine where it is folded at the joints there are double layers of paper that can become bulky if you don't allow for their thickness.

*25* Transfer the spine measurement to the wrapper. Use the center pencil mark to center the spine measurement, then erase the center mark.

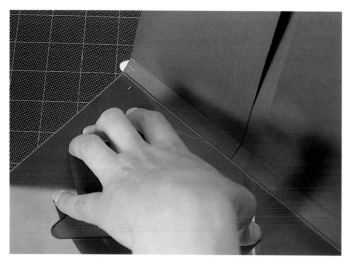

*26* Line a plastic triangle up against the head fold and along each mark at the spine and hold the triangle firmly with one hand while you score and fold the wrapper up against the triangle with a bone folder in the other hand.

*27* Transfer the width measurement to the wrapper. Measure from the spine edge out.

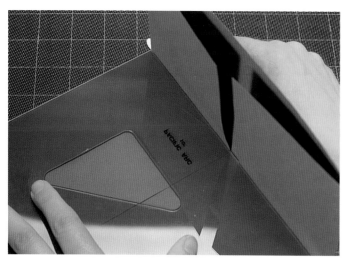

*28* Score and fold the flaps on both front and back. Trim the flaps so they are even and square.

*29* Slide the first three pages into the end flap of the wrapper at both the front and the back. You may have to stand the book up on the work surface and jiggle it around a bit to get the pages in neatly. If you have made the cover a little too short, you can take those first and last three pages out and trim them down a little so that they will slide in.

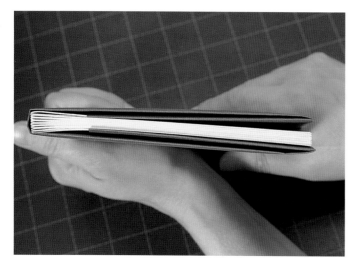

*30* There tends to be a lot of air inside when you first make up this book. Place another book or some sort of light weight on top overnight. Keep the weight away from the spine, which can be crushed because it is only folded paper.

*Hint*

*Cut two pieces of lightweight board so they are a little shorter and not quite as wide as the front and back of the wrapper. Slide them in either under the pages you put into the wrapper or further in under the folds of the front and back cover of the wrapper.*

# GALLERY *of* IDEAS

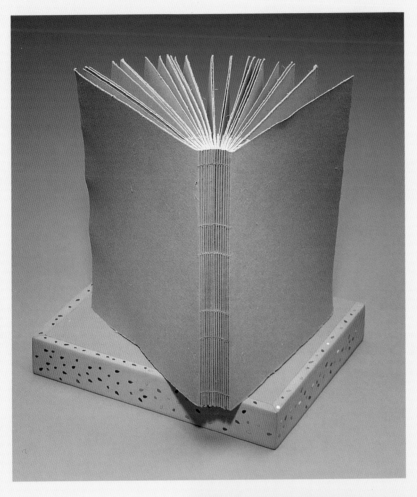

### Allen Wedding Album
Gabrielle Fox
handmade paper and thread
12" × 9" (30.5cm × 22.9cm)

Different colored threads can just be seen running along the four rows of stitching. The paper was so beautiful I left it without a cover and made a slipcase to protect the album.

### Train Log
*(codex and scroll format)*
Hedi Kyle
crimped exotic paper, leather, Firenze paper soaked in coffee and painted, waxed linen thread, Amtrak paper towels, wooden stick covered with Japanese paper, colored pencil writing, computer-generated text rolled up
6½" × 6½" (16.5cm × 16.5cm)

The sewing structure of this book is different than that of project nine. I included it just to give you inspiration.

# ONE PIECE SLIPCASE

This slipcase—made with a single piece of card folded and glued at the head and tail—is easy to make for protection of any book in your collection.

The flaps, which fold in at the front and back, form an air cushion which keeps the book in place. The double layer of card all around makes the slipcase strong, while the card's flexibility enables you to put your hand inside to pull the book out, rather than shaking it onto the floor.

This slipcase was designed to protect books without going to great expense in time or materials.

The disastrous Florence floods of 1966 brought skilled individuals from all around the world who worked for years conserving the treasures that could be saved from the water. The gathering of book and paper conservators who worked on the books and documents created a new focus and approach to the traditional skills. As a result, there is ongoing research and experimentation both in caring for old books and making new ones. Many interesting structures, like this one, are a result of that work in Italy.

## WHAT YOU'LL NEED

- one 20" × 30¾" (50.8cm × 78.1cm), 140 lb. (150gsm) piece of Canford Card by Daler-Rowney in Champagne

- bone folder

- cutting mat

- large triangle

- pencil

- PVA glue, brush and container

- ruler or strips of paper for measuring

- scrap paper

- small craft knife

- spring dividers

- straightedge

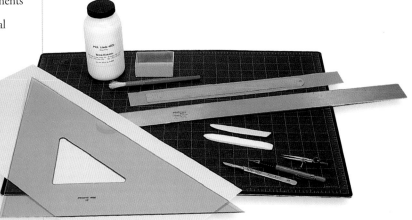

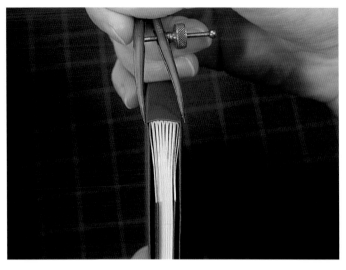

*1* Measure the depth of the book you wish to insert in the slipcase at its thickest point. This is usually the spine.

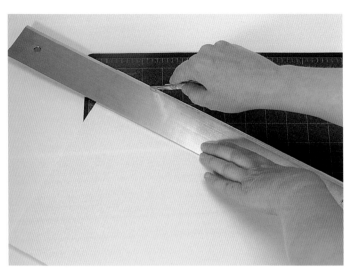

*2* Make a straight cut across the top edge of the card or heavy paper with a straightedge and craft knife.

*3* Mark your book's depth in several places along the length of the card.

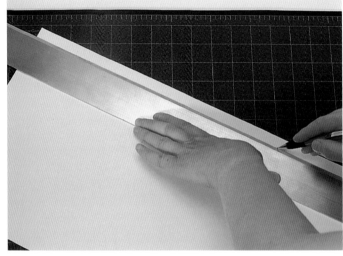

*4* Draw a straight line using those marks.

*5* Fold the card gently in half lengthwise and mark the center point on the card.

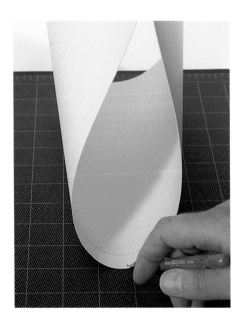

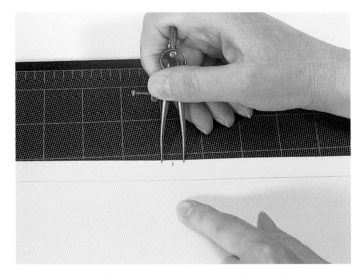

*6* Transfer the depth measurement to the card using the center pencil mark as a guide. Erase the center mark.

*7* Line a plastic triangle up with the top edge and against the spine marks, one at a time, and draw a line with a pencil.

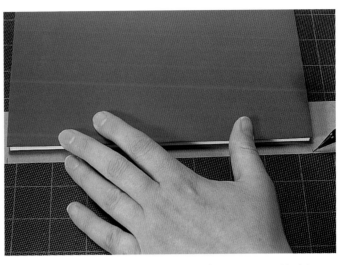

*8* Measure the height of the book. Don't be too stingy with this measurement or the book won't fit into the slipcase.

*9* Transfer this measurement to the card. Measure from the top pencil line down. Mark this measurement in several places along the length of the card.

*10* Line up your straightedge along the marks and draw a pencil line.

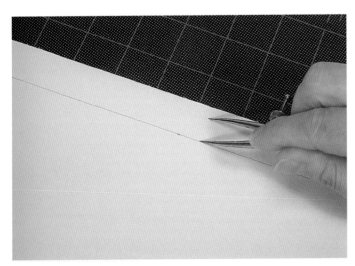

*11* Mark the spine measurement—used first at the top of the card—to the bottom of the card. Measure from the last line, the height measurement, down.

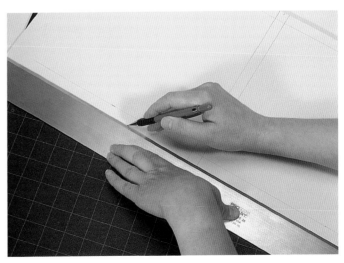

*12* Line the straightedge up along these marks and trim off any excess card.

*13* Measure the width of the book.

*14* Transfer the width measurement to the card. Measure from the spine line out.

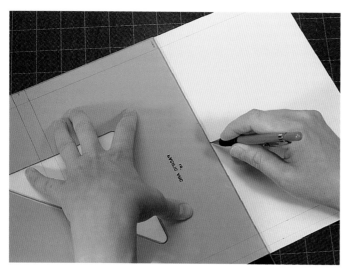

*15* Draw a pencil line along the mark you have just made for the width of your book. A plastic triangle lined up against one of the horizontal lines you have drawn can help to keep these lines square in relation to the rest of slipcase.

*16* Repeat the measurement on the other side and draw a line along that mark.

*17* The next measurement is just a little less than the width of the book. It can be as little as ⅟₁₆ inch (0.16cm) less in width than the book.

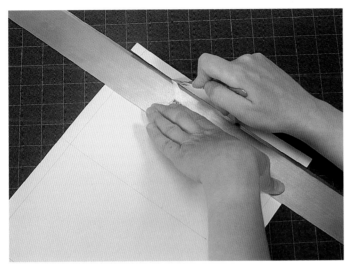

**18** Transfer this measurement to the card on both the right and the left. Measure the distance from the last lines you made, which were the width lines. This last measurement drawn from top to bottom is for the flaps which tuck inside the slipcase. If they are the same width as the slipcase, they are likely to jam up and not fold down flat inside with the book. Cut along the last lines you have drawn, to the left and right, and your slipcase will be ready to be cut and folded.

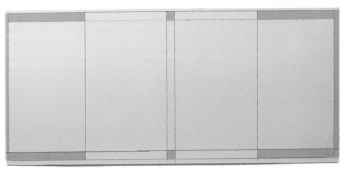

This is how the card will look when all lines are drawn. The shaded areas will be cut away in the following steps.

**19** Trim off, at top and bottom, right and left, all four slices of card. These pieces are the segments drawn in at the top and far corners of the card. Cut first along the little line from the top edge to the first line. This line is the last line you drew going out to the left and right. Detach the strip of card by cutting along the first line and last lines drawn from top to bottom.

**20** Moving in from the left and the right, cut along the next line as far as the first line from top to bottom. Next, take a little piece off the corner of the tabs you have made in the middle. This is just mitering the corners so that everything will fold in easily.

**21** Score the slipcase along the lines with your bone folder.

$22$ Fold the slipcase along the scored lines.

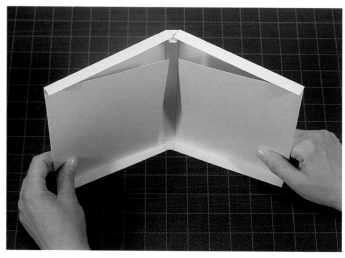

$23$ Check to see you have cut and folded everything before you begin to glue the slipcase together.

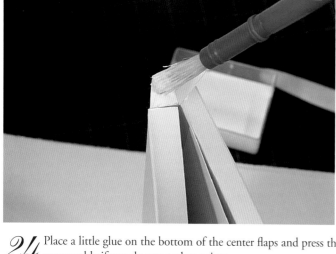

$24$ Place a little glue on the bottom of the center flaps and press them down. It is more manageable if you do one end at a time.

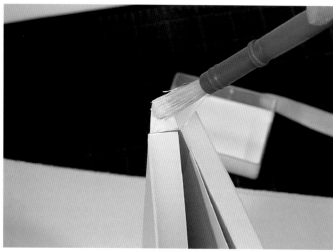

$25$ Lift up the righthand flap and glue all along the edge. Hold it upright and gently rub the top flap down over the tab and lefthand flap. Glue down one end at a time.

# GALLERY *of* IDEAS

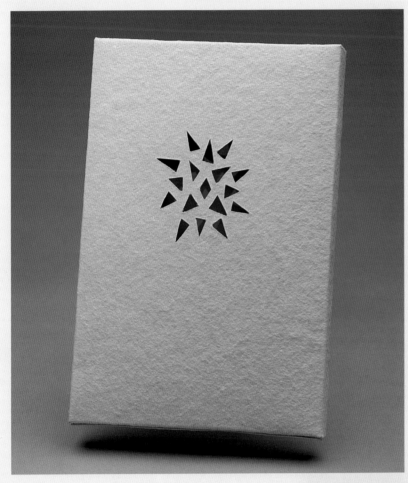

*Stars*
Gabrielle Fox
handmade and flocked paper
7" × 4½" (17.8cm × 11.4cm)

The different colored lining of the inside flap
of this slipcase is revealed through the cutout
pattern.

*Thin Butterfly*
Gabrielle Fox
paper-backed book cloth
4" × 10" (10.2cm × 25.4cm)

The stability of the paper backing
on this Japanese book cloth
enables you to use it as you
would a lightweight card.

# SIMPLE PORTFOLIO

The portfolio is a basic container which was probably in existence long before any portable book was made.

This portfolio is very simple. The main point to remember is to keep your lines straight and square in relation to one another. The portfolio will then close well and protect whatever you put inside it.

You can make this portfolio to contain a book or a collection of loose drawings or pages. Some variations you may wish to try:

- Cover the portfolio in a different type of material rather than just the cloth I've used.
- Turn in the edges of the covering material to make it look more finished.
- Build it a bit like a box and add ribbons or velcro to close it.

Look at some of the examples in the gallery for other ideas to modify this basic idea. This simple version is just a good place to begin.

## WHAT YOU'LL NEED

- Two pieces of cloth lined with paper which are approximately 22" × 20" (55.9cm × 50.8cm). This cloth is available from most bookbinding suppliers and comes in different styles and colors. The paper lining allows you to see the lines you draw much more easily.

- One 15" × 16" (38.1cm × 40.6cm) sheet of four-ply, conservation-quality mat board, or other 1/16" to 1/8" (0.16cm × 0.3cm) thick board. You will cut this into five pieces for the portfolio and four scraps of board for measuring. The grain of the board must go from head to tail of the portfolio.

- bone folder
- cutting mat
- heavy craft knife
- large triangle

- pencil
- PVA glue, brush and container
- scrap paper
- small craft knife
- small L-square or triangle
- spring dividers
- straightedge

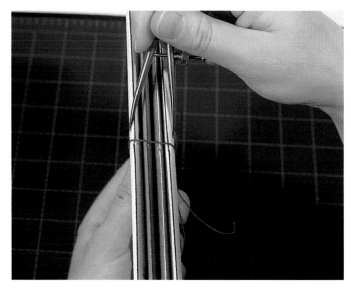

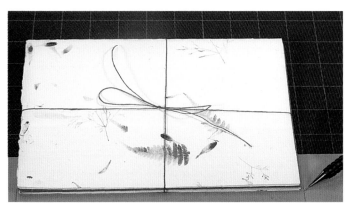

*1* Measure the depth of the book, books or papers you would like to keep in the portfolio. I'm using four single sections I have sewn into covers made of different pieces of handmade paper with different colors of linen thread. Since I want to put all four books in the portfolio, I'm measuring them as a unit.

*2* Measure the height and width of your item(s). These measurements should be fairly precise. Be sure you measure to the longest and widest point; my books weren't all exactly the same size.

*3* Check the board you are using to be certain you are working with the grain going from head to tail and that the corner you begin measuring from is square. Cut out five pieces of board for the portfolio: Make the center piece and the left and top flaps the same height and width as the items you measured in step two. Make the right flap the same height and two-thirds the width as step two. Make the two flaps at the top and bottom just less (⅛ inch [0.3cm] approximately) than the height and the width of step two. Also keep four scraps of this board for measuring the portfolio covering.

*4* With a pencil, draw a line diagonally across the top two corners on the top and bottom flaps and across the two left corners on the right side flap. These lines are exact guides to cut off these corners with a small craft knife or scalpel and a small straightedge.

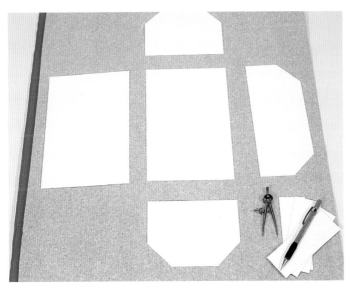

*5* Place the pieces you've cut in their approximate positions on your fabric to get a sense of the spacing and where to begin marking for the center board.

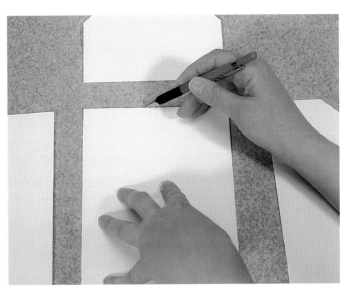

*6* Trace lightly all around the center board.

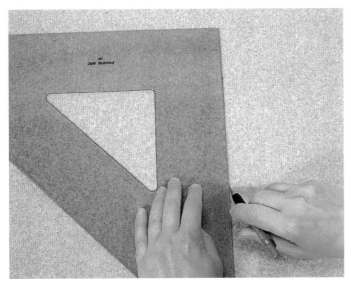

*7* Remove the boards and use a plastic triangle to mark out exactly where the center board will be positioned when you glue it to the cloth.

*8* Place the center board back down using the pencil marks you have just drawn.

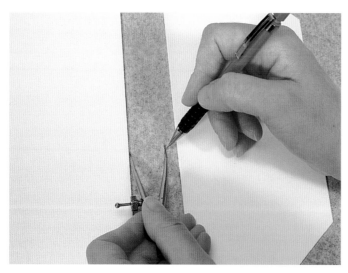

*9* To the right of the center board, mark the depth of the spine (I've set my spring dividers to this measurement) plus the thickness of two pieces of scrap board.

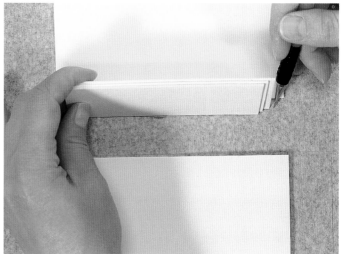

*10* Make a mark from the edge of the center board at the top and bottom at a distance which is the depth of the spine plus the thickness of three pieces of scrap board.

*11* The distance of the top flap, which is to the left of the center board, will be the depth of the book plus four board thicknesses.

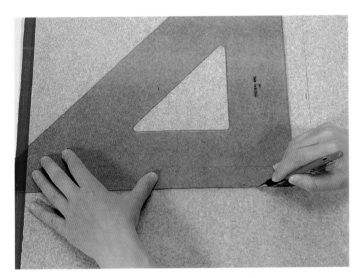

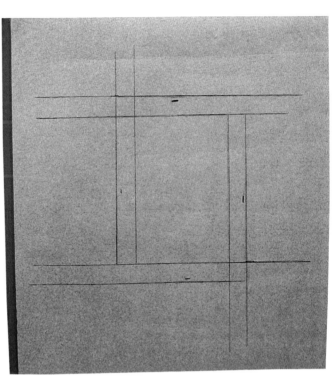

*12* Remove all the pieces of board and carefully draw all the lines using a plastic square or other straightedge which will enable you to keep everything square in relation to one another.

*13* When you are finished, this is the grid you will have drawn.

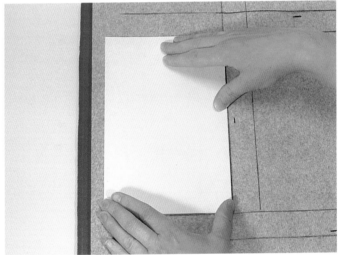

*14* Begin gluing the pieces to the fabric from left to right. Stipple the glue on the back of the board and then position the board onto the cloth between the lines you have drawn.

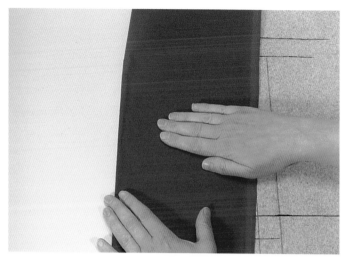

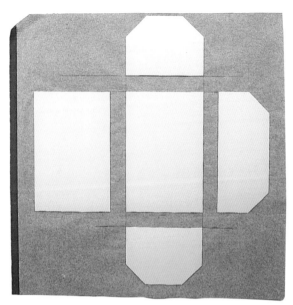

*15* Fold the cloth over so that you can check there are no air bubbles, then smooth the cloth down from the outside. Working from left to right (or right to left, if you prefer) makes it a little easier to line the boards up and fold the portfolio over to check the outside.

*16* Glue down one piece at a time until all five boards are in place.

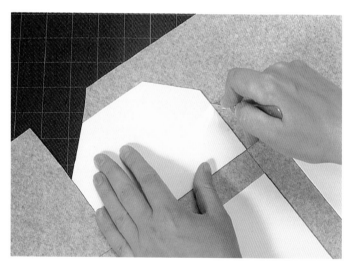

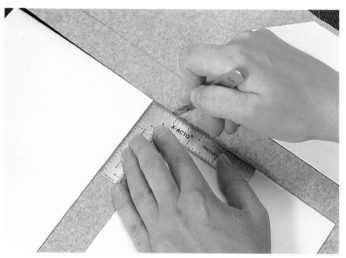

*17* Wait for about ten minutes to allow the glue to dry a bit. If you begin cutting too soon, you may pull the damp cloth and get a rough edge. Cut straight through the cloth along the outside edges of the portfolio with a small craft knife or scalpel blade.

*18* A metal or plastic L-square or triangle will help to keep the cut line straight in between the boards where there is only cloth.

*19* When you have cut around the whole portfolio, you are ready to line it.

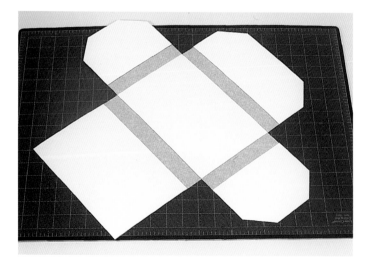

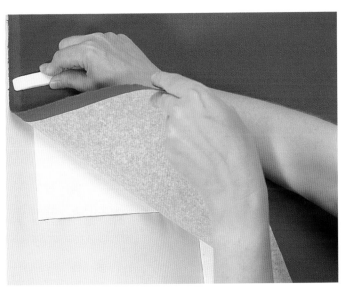

*20* Remember to place scrap paper under the portfolio before you begin to apply the glue. Stipple the glue onto the portfolio and work from one side to the other.

*21* Lay the cloth down in stages from one side of the portfolio to the other.

*22* Work the cloth across and in between the boards with your hands and bone folder. If you rub the cloth against the edges of the boards in the spaces in between, there will be a much neater appearance and fit. Don't panic, the cloth has some give. Don't rub the cloth over the outside edges. The cloth at the outside edges should be just flat on the boards.

*23* Wait for about ten minutes to let the inside dry a little before trimming the portfolio lining just as you trimmed the covering earlier.

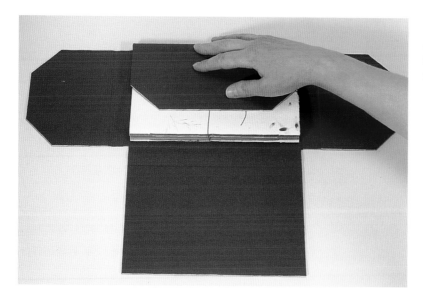

*24* The portfolio will probably take several hours to dry completely. When it is dry, place the books inside and fold the long thin flap over first.

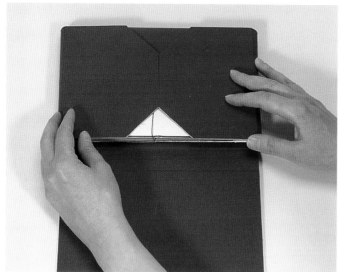

*25* Fold the two end flaps next.

*26* Fold the full-sized flap last.

# GALLERY *of* IDEAS

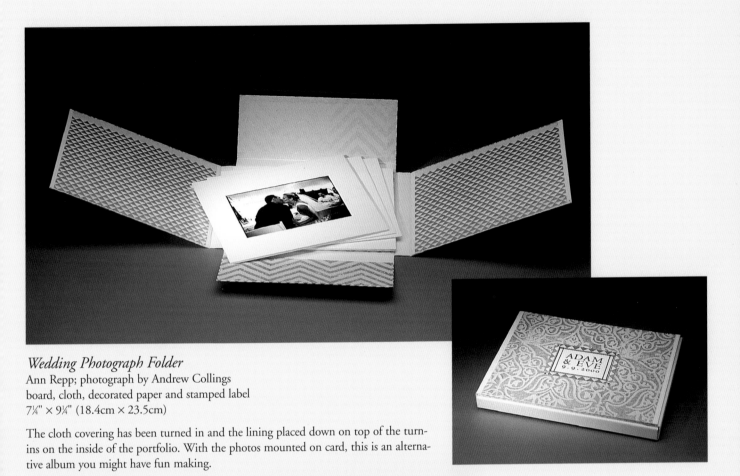

## *Wedding Photograph Folder*
Ann Repp; photograph by Andrew Collings
board, cloth, decorated paper and stamped label
7¼" × 9¼" (18.4cm × 23.5cm)

The cloth covering has been turned in and the lining placed down on top of the turn-ins on the inside of the portfolio. With the photos mounted on card, this is an alternative album you might have fun making.

## *Agricultural Notation*
binding by Cris Clair Takacs
board, cloth and paper
8¾" × 5¾" (22.2cm × 14.6cm)

The side walls are rigid and built in place before the two flaps with their own rigid walls are attached to the base. This is more complicated, but may get you thinking about the possibilities.

# SUPPLIERS

**AIKO'S ART MATERIALS IMPORT, INC.**
3347 N. Clark Street
Chicago, IL 60657
*Phone* (312) 404-5600
*Fax* (312) 404-5919

**BOOKMAKERS INTERNATIONAL**
6701B Lafayette Avenue
Riverdale, MD 20737
*Phone* (301) 927-7787
*Fax* (301) 927-7715
*E-mail* bookmakers@aol.com

**CAVE PAPER**
1334 6th Street N.E.
Minneapolis, MN 55413
*Phone* ( 612) 788-9440 or (612) 378-2696
*E-mail* amanda_degener@mcad.edu

**COLOPHON BOOK ARTS SUPPLY, INC.**
3611 Ryan Street SE
Lacey, WA 98503
*Phone* (360) 459-2940
*Fax* (360) 459-2945
*E-mail* colophon@olywa.net

**CREATIVE FIBERS**
5416 Penn Avenue South
Minneapolis, MN 55419
*Phone* (612) 927-8307

**DOLPHIN PAPERS**
1125 Brookside Avenue G-900
Indianapolis, Indiana 46202
*Phone* (800) 346-2770
*Local phone* (317) 634-0506
*Fax* (317) 634-1370

**THE HARCOURT BINDERY**
51 Melcher Street
Boston, Massachusetts 02210
*Phone* (617) 542-5858 or
(617) 451-9058

**KATE'S PAPERIE**
561 Broadway
New York, NY 10012
*Phone* (212) 941-9816
*Fax* (212) 941-0194

**LEHMANN BINDERY**
1421 Vale Terrace Drive
Vista, CA 92084
*Phone* (760) 758-4142
*Fax* (760) 631-1869
*Web site* www.ixpres.com/lehmannbindery

**ANNE MUIR MARBLING**
1 St. Algar's Yard
West Woodlands
Frome, Somerset BA11 5ER
England
*Phone* 01985-844786

**PAPER SOURCE, INC.**
232 W. Chicago Avenue
Chicago, IL 60610
*Phone* (312) 337-0798
*Fax* (312) 337-0741

**ROYAL MAIL PHILATELIC BUREAU**
20 Brandon Street
Edinburgh EH3 0HN
Scotland
*Web site* www.royalmail.co.uk
*Phone* 01345 740740

**ROYALWOOD LTD.**
Basketweaving & Caning Supplies
517 Woodville Road
Mansfield, Ohio 44907
*Phone* (800) 526-1630
*Local phone* (419) 526-1630
*Fax* (888) 526-1618
(419) 526-1618
*E-mail* roybilkat@worldnet.att.net
*Web site* www.bright.net/~roylwood/

**LA PAPETERIE SAINT-GILLES**
304 rue Felix Antoine
Savard, CP 40
St. Joseph de la Rive, Quebec
Canada G0A 3Y0
*Phone* (418) 635-2430

**TALAS**
568 Broadway
New York, NY 10002-1996
*Phone* (212) 219-0770
*Fax* (212) 219-0735

**TWINROCKER HANDMADE PAPER**
100 East Third
Brookston, IN 47923
*Phone* (800) 757-TWIN(8946)
*Fax* (765) 563-TWIN(8946)
*Web site* www.twinrocker.com

**UNIVERSITY PRODUCTS, INC.**
P.O. Box 101
517 Main Street
Holyoke, MA 01041
*Phone* (800) 336-4847

*For further information about bookbinding, classes and suppliers:*

**GUILD OF BOOKWORKERS**
521 Fifth Avenue
New York, NY 10175
Newsletter
http://palimpsest.stanford.edu/byorg/gbw
Library listing
www.lib.uiowa.edu/spec-coll-NARRFIN.htm

**THE CANADIAN BOOKBINDERS AND BOOK ARTISTS GUILD**
176 John Street, Suite 309
Toronto, Ontario M5T IX5
*Phone* (416) 581-1071
*Fax* (905) 851-6029

# CONTRIBUTORS

**MARYLINE POOLE ADAMS**
*The King's Breakfast* © Maryline Poole Adams, p. 67
*Jabberwocky* © Maryline Poole Adams, p. 51

**CHARLES ALEXANDER**
Chax Press
101 W. 6th St., No. 6
Tuscson, AZ 85701
chax@theriver.com
http://alexwritdespub.com/chax
*Zootaxy* © Charles Alexander; illustration © Cynthia Miller, p. 83

**ERIC ALSTROM**
Hanover, NH
*Untitled Blank Book* © Eric Alstrom, p. 95

**REBECCA SAADY BINGHAM**
6805 Forest Hill Drive
University Park, MD 20782
rbingham@octagamm.com
*Erté Maquettes* © Rebecca Saady Bingham, p. 95

**JOHN CUTRONE**
Red Wagon Press
*Woods Story* © John Cutrone, p. 75

**WILLIAM DRENDEL**
*Apart From Being Flippant, What Are You Doing Here?* © William Drendel, p. 41
*Tanna Touva Where Are You?* © William Drendel, p. 126

**EDWARD H. HUTCHINS**
Editions
PO Box 895
Cairo, NY 12413
www.artistbooks.com
*Tunnel O' Love* © Edward H. Hutchins, p. 21

**PAUL JOHNSON**
*Peep Show Book* © Paul Johnson, p. 21

**KATE KERN**
Cincinnati, OH
KMKern@compuserve.com
*Janus* © Kate Kern, p. 33

**ELIZABETH KOFFEL**
*Pretty in Pink* © Elizabeth Koffel, p. 21

**HEDI KYLE**
hkyle@amphilsoc.org
*Hawaiian Scroll, 1996* © Hedi Kyle; photograph © Paul Warchol, p. 83
*Train Log, 1996* © Hedi Kyle; photograph © Paul Warchol p. 105

**EMILY MARTIN**
emartin@avalon.net
www.emilymartin.com
(319) 338-7266
*Yes, Please and No, No, Never* © Emily Martin, p. 51

**ANN MUIR**
Ann Muir Marbling
1 St. Algar's Yard
West Woodlands
Frome, Somerset, BA11 5ER
United Kingdom
hand-marbled paper in projects two and five © Ann Muir

**SUSAN NAYLOR**
Cincinnati, OH
*Jacob's Ladder* © Susan Naylor, p. 51

**ANN REPP**
30 W. Hubbard
Chicago, IL 60610
(312) 494-1730
*Wedding Photograph Folder* © Ann Repp, photograph shown in folder © Andrew Collings, p. 123

**MARGARET RHEIN**
Terrapin Paper Mill
2318 Nicholson Avenue
Cincinnati, OH 45217
paperpeg@aol.com
(513) 662-9382
*Garden Mix* © Margaret Rhein, p. 40

**MARIANNE ROGENSKI**
*Two Beads* © Marianne Rogenski, p. 95

**CRIS CLAIR TAKACS**
Books Bound & Repaired
112 Park Avenue
Chardon, OH 44024
(440) 286-9773
*Agricultural Notation* © Cris Clair Takacs, p. 123

**DIANNE EWELL WEISS**
The Figment Press
300 Montford Avenue
Mill Valley, CA 94941
*1996 Miniature Book Conclave–San Francisco* © Dianne Ewell Weiss, p. 67

**CAROLYN WHITESEL**
Yellowbird Editions
1652 First Avenue
Cincinnati, OH 45205
*City* © Carolyn Whitesel, p. 33
*Spider Poems* © Gray Zeitz, Larkspur Press; text © Jeff Worley; binding © Carolyn Whitesel, p. 74
*Never Mind* © Carolyn Whitesel, p.126

**VIRGINIA WISNIEWSKI**
*Green & Pink Paste Paper* © Virginia Wisniewski, p. 41

**DOROTHY A. YULE**
Left Coast Press
5723 Picardy Drive
Oakland, CA 94605
*Souvenirs of Great Cities* © Dorothy A. Yule; illustrations © Susan Hunt Yule, p. 33

# GALLERY *of* IDEAS

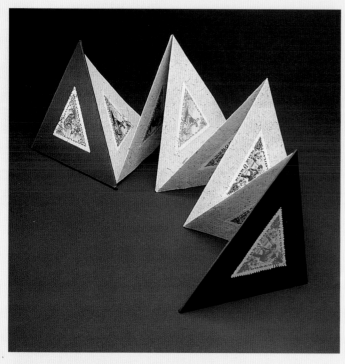

*Tanna Touva Where Are You?*
William Drendel
Bhutanese paper, Tanna Touva stamps between triangular boards;
3" × 3" × 4" (7.6cm × 7.6cm × 10.2cm)

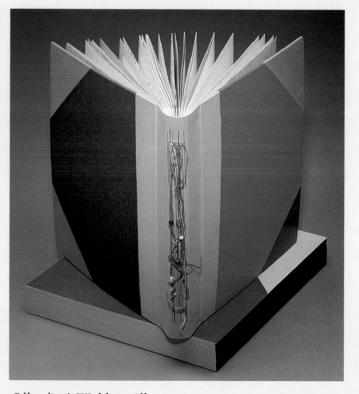

*Olberding's Wedding Album*
Gabrielle Fox
multicolor paper laminated to light card and sewn into leather and
cloth-covered cover; 10½" × 10" × 1⅜" (26.7cm × 25.4cm × 3.5cm)

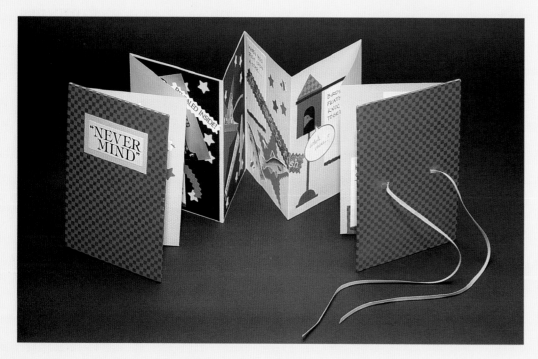

*Never Mind*
Carolyn Whitesel
accordion with collage text and
paper-covered boards with ribbon
closure; 4¼" × 6¼" (10.8cm ×
15.9cm)

# Index